The Dark Art of Pricing

The Dark Art of Pricing

Deliberately Pricing for Profit

Andrew Gregson BA, MA, MSc (Econ)

Self-Counsel Press
(a division of)
International Self-Counsel Press Ltd.
Canada   USA

Self-Counsel Press acknowledges the financial support of the Government of Canada for our publishing activities. Canada

Printed in Canada.

First edition: 2019

Library and Archives Canada Cataloguing in Publication

Title: The dark art of pricing : deliberately pricing for profit / Andrew Gregson.

Names: Gregson, Andrew, author.

Series: Self-Counsel business series.

Description: Series statement: Business series

Identifiers: Canadiana (print) 20190148942 | Canadiana (ebook) 20190148969 | ISBN 9781770403154 (softcover) | ISBN 9781770405028 (EPUB) | ISBN 9781770405035 (Kindle)

Subjects: LCSH: Pricing. | LCSH: Profit.

Classification: LCC HF5416.5 .G74 2019 | DDC 658.8/16—dc23

Self-Counsel Press
(a division of)
International Self-Counsel Press Ltd.

North Vancouver, BC
Canada

Bellingham, WA
USA

Contents

Checklists

Worksheets

Notice to Readers

Laws are constantly changing. Every effort is made to keep this publication as current as possible. However, the author, the publisher, and the vendor of this book make no representations or warranties regarding the outcome or the use to which the information in this book is put and are not assuming any liability for any claims, losses, or damages arising out of the use of this book. The reader should not rely on the author or the publisher of this book for any professional advice. Please be sure that you have the most recent edition.

Acknowledgments

I am dedicating this book to my father, Charles William Gregson, who passed away December 2, 2015, and to whom I owe a debt of gratitude for teaching me that an unbroken record of success is always a result of doing nothing. Most of the pricing errors I refer to in this book have been committed by me. We learn by doing and failing.

To my patient wife, Judith, who would prefer that we travel but has endured my passion for proselytizing that pricing is the final frontier of profit engineering.

I owe a debt of thanks to people who have read parts of the book and given back useful critiques: Richard Turley of Okanagan College, and Larry Widmer of Community Futures of the Okanagan.

I particularly owe thanks to all of the employees, clients, colleagues, and bosses who have listened to me over the years and offered their experience and further insight, all of which resulted in this more prescriptive book than my first.

Finally, I owe a big thanks to Self-Counsel Press and the encouragement they have always offered, and the chance they have taken with this work.

Preface

I have spent years consulting on profitability to small- and medium-sized businesses in North America. What I learned in doing this was that their experiences were not that different from my own, as I have started and owned five businesses, including two franchises. Many of these businesses struggled to generate enough wealth to make retirement for the owners a comfortable proposition. Far too many struggled just to pay the rent, payroll, or taxes. I know that they fought hard to try to be profitable, cutting fat and often slicing into corporate muscle to keep costs down.

Too often, the owners are the last ones to be paid.

Every business owner I worked with knew everything about the supply side of their business equation; they knew their sales processes and their costs. However, they could not grasp the other half of the transaction: the demand. In particular, how this applies to pricing and its role in profit and wealth generation.

I have called this book *The Dark Art of Pricing* because for many the process of determining price is akin to boiling eye of newt in a cauldron surrounded by wicked witches. Pricing is not magic, any more than selling is magic.

Finding the right pricing strategy is, like developing a sales program, work. It takes testing and tweaking. But the "how" and "why" are buried in corporate vaults and academic journals, almost inaccessible to the average business owner. My purpose in this book is to take those ideas and make them available to business owners so that they too can earn the profits they deserve.

This book builds upon the foundation I laid in my first book, *Pricing Strategies for Small Business* (Self-Counsel Press, 2008). After ten years of research and preaching that pricing is the last frontier of profit making, I needed to update my book with all that I have learned. Hence this book is more process driven and certainly grittier.

You will notice many references to my personal business experience in this book. When I lectured at Cape Breton University to MBA and BBA students, one of the attendees asked why I knew so intimately how pricing failed. My response was that I had made all the mistakes I talked about. Making mistakes is normal, but failing to learn from them is unfortunate.

What I wish for all business owners is that they find a way to charge what they are really worth, to drive larger profits, to build wealth, and to attract a buyer when the time comes to retire to a sandy beach. I hope this book helps them do just that.

Introduction: Why Is Pricing Important?

Pricing should be of the utmost importance to business owners because it is possible to use price strategies to engineer a deliberate profit.

You can drive sales and cut costs. Your accountant can tell you how to cut costs. Sales trainers can help you improve sales.

What is often mostly ignored is pricing, and pricing is, in my opinion, the final frontier of profit generation.

I tend to slam conventional pricing methods hard because it leads to mediocre results. Later on, I will offer some tried and tested pricing strategies used by companies such as Apple and DuPont. I will also explain the importance of knowing how to "sell your price," that being an immediate step to more sales and higher profits. My focus in this book is on value pricing because without value on the table, why would anyone pay your price? I will also offer two extended case studies about Return on Investment (ROI) pricing and price banding.

To make this book work for you, the reader and business owner, we must first establish that most pricing systems produce mediocre results and leave money on the table. Let's discuss some common myths.

1. Five Common Pricing Myths

At the bar and over the phone, business owners recycle old myths about their businesses and their industry in an attempt to simplify and understand their circumstances, but the myths do not bear much close scrutiny. Here are five deconstructed myths.

1.1 All my competitors buy better so they can sell more cheaply, and that explains my poor sales

It is unlikely that all of a business's competitors are able to buy better and sell more cheaply. Globalization of supply chains has made it simple for even owners of small stores to source well. The suppliers play games, of course, with volume discounts, rebates, and other sales devices to push up sales. But, to blame the supply chain for poor sales performance is just deflecting attention from other business problems.

1.2 Every customer who says we are too expensive is right

There are customers for whom free would be too expensive. Remember too, that sticker shock can be a buyer's strategy to get you to lower your price. There are some customers who buy on price alone but they need to be gently pointed in the direction of a competitor. These customers are no respecters of the value you offer. In general, enough customers will buy what they value.

1.3 If sales drop, then it is the fault of my high prices

Depending on how many items you're selling, it is unlikely that all your prices are poorly positioned. Most regular buyers of a particular product or service can recall ten prices only. That appears to be the maximum number of prices we can remember and then only through constant reinforcement. So, in a store selling a 1,000 items, as many as 990 things have no reference price in the mind of the buyer. Of course this applies to retail or distributors and wholesalers, but could also apply in the narrower range of the contracting world. Elaborating your offering with value propositions and add-ons for concrete work, say, helps you use that power of ten.

1.4 My invoice costs are the only factors that determine prices

Profits are determined by a whole host of factors. Among them are programs such as those involving volume discounts, 30 days to pay, free delivery, free installation, free support, and free add-ons. These factors and programs drive up costs but all too typically are not accounted for when building a price. These off-invoice costs are part of the price waterfall that erodes profits. See the Castle Battery case study in Chapter 13.

1.5 The price is the only factor that influences a sale

Price is not the only factor that influences a sale. With items of fashion or taste, higher prices are associated with better quality or social standing. There are cheaper sneakers than the ones demanded by teenagers so that they are seen as cool in their social circles. A Hyundai will get you to work just as easily as a Mercedes. Diamond rings would not be the symbol of undying love if they sold for $4.95, would they?

2. What This Book Is About

This book is the culmination of research and experience first incorporated into my book *Pricing Strategies for Small Business* (Self-Counsel Press, 2008), and then augmented by a subsequent decade of talking to business owners, students, and colleagues as they try to apply my ideas.

The purpose of this book is to present pricing as a tool to increase profits. Yes, big companies have pricing strategies that they nurture, protect, and aggressively use. But gaining an insight into what they are doing is almost impossible. Pricing is a tool underresearched, little understood, and underused by small businesses. If you want to cry into your martini and blame someone else for your business problems, go ahead. If you want to succeed, developing an innovative pricing strategy is the most powerful way to improve profit and build your customer base.

Pricing is part of marketing and not accounting and therefore a strategy should be born out of an individual business's marketing principles.

If you are a business owner, you already know your costs, but what you may not know is the upper limit of your price and profit band. I am not writing about gouging or ripping off customers. What I want you, the business owner, to understand is that people are willing to pay for quality, convenience, and service — but only if they are clearly articulated.

This book is not about increasing your prices but finding that sweet spot where you become the price leader because you are the best in your industry or area, and the go-to company because of the value you offer.

If you are in a hurry, you may wish to look first at Chapter 1, The Quick Fix, for an immediate boost in your ability to command the right price. Of course, if you follow my advice you should get a prompt return on your investment in this book!

Chapter 1
The Quick Fix

If your company is facing profitability problems today, this is a quick fix.

How quickly could you double your profits through extra sales alone? For most of us, doubling profits means doubling sales. Could you do that instantly or at least quickly?

How quickly could you double your profits from cost cutting alone? Just the thought of trying to do that should make you shiver.

But, you could change your prices tonight!

I am not an advocate of simply raising your prices without some justification. Typically reasonable justifications would be a rise in the cost of living, inflation, or simply that costs have risen for the industry. Most businesses could manage to raise prices by a mere 5 percent without losing or even alarming customers.

Rather, I would expect that businesses raise their prices after finding a solid competitive edge that demonstrates beyond the shadow of a doubt that they have put value on the table for the customer to see, taste, or touch.

Occasionally, however, there is a case to be made for a simple price hike. Businesses in serious trouble and in danger of collapse may be helped by this short chapter.

In my years of research, I learned that once, a sample of customers had to choose between fictitious, outwardly identical floor polish products, the only difference being the price. Fifty-seven percent of people chose the more expensive product.

Most small businesses in North America have a bottom line, before tax, of 5 to 10 percent. That means that the costs of goods and services provided plus the cost of administering the company come to a princely 90 to 95 percent. In Figure 1 this is illustrated for an imaginary million-dollar company.

BEFORE		
Revenue	$1,000,000	100%
Direct and Admin Costs	$950,000	95%
Profit	$50,000	5%

Figure 1: Typical $1 Million Business's Bottom Line

Let us suppose however, that you were to increase prices and do nothing else. Most companies could raise prices by 5 percent without customers leaving.

Let's look at the impact of merely making that one change in Figure 2. Make no other changes, no increases in costs or administration, and you can see that the 5 percent extra drops promptly to the bottom line. Just 5 percent more in price effectively doubles the bottom line in this example.

AFTER		
Revenue	$1,000,000	100%
Price Increase	$50,000	5%
Direct and Admin Costs	$950,000	
Profit	$100,000	10%

Figure 2: Typical 5 Percent Price Increase to $1 Million Business's Bottom Line

No other recommendation I could ever make to you and your company could double your profits so quickly.

Chapter 2
How to Present Your New Prices (Or, How to Sell Your Dream Price)

In this marketplace, customers are relentless at hunting down the lowest possible price. To be completely fair, quality and value come in a poor second if you have limited funds to spend. But bargain hunters come in two flavors. First, there are the customers who will drive across town to save a dollar because they need that dollar. For the rest however, they will trade dollars for quality, convenience, or perceived value.

Therefore, the fastest way to improve profits is to learn how to sell your DREAM price. The following sections give 18 guidelines to follow to do just that.

1. Prepare for Sticker Shock

For some customers, feigning sticker shock is part of the game of fishing for a lower price. Acknowledge it, but move on. Do not offer a discount!

2. Deal with Objections You Know about Early and Head-on

It is wise here to prepare the customer early. In the 1980s, Nescafé sales representatives approached potential customers with the opening line, "I am here to tell you why you should buy the most expensive instant coffee on the market." This is a useful and disarming statement that can be adapted to almost any industry. According to its own website as of March 2019, Nestlé today sells more than 5,500 cups of Nescafé instant coffee every second with different varieties catering to different tastes and preferences around the globe.

3. Keep Your Price to the End

Customers who press for a price right out of the gate are not interested in anything else. They have to be told politely and bluntly that if price is the only consideration, then this company offers more that you may wish to pay for.

The better approach to persuading the customers they want to pay your price is to ask a lot of questions that demonstrate that your company knows what it is talking about and has the best interests of the customers at heart.

If you are working with a business customer, at some point the question of what happened to the last supplier has to be asked. This is the killer question because it tells you the sensitive areas. The best response to a customer story of complaints about prior contractors is "Yes, we had that problem too, but we fixed that a while ago." Again you are demonstrating empathy with the customer and industry knowledge without slamming the competition.

Even if you have the lowest price in town, the customer may still have doubts about quality, so a presentation that satisfies all these doubts may have to be made before price is discussed.

Sales are first about building a relationship and then providing value before offering a price. Leave price to the end and build a collaborative relationship with the customer and you improve the chances of getting your dream price.

4. Start with a Big Ask

A chemical salesman I employed had a successful career selling cleaning chemicals in western Canada. His home office was decorated with award after award testifying to his considerable abilities. When I asked him how it was done in a commodity business like that, he told me the secret was to extol the virtues of the product and its benefits. Then he would ask the customers for an order of one skid of four 45-gallon drums. Sometimes the answer was yes, but mostly it was no.

If the answer was no, he would acknowledge that this was a little too much and ask how much the customer wanted. Usually, the answer was one drum or perhaps a half skid of cases.

The point was that selling one gallon first and then trying to get the quantity up was a losing strategy that would not have earned him all these shiny awards, but pushing for a larger sale sometimes got the larger sale, and sometimes got at least a smaller one.

5. Frame Your Price

Framing and reference pricing are features of a sales presentation that place your offering in the competitive hierarchy by elaborating non-price features and benefits.

Your offering could gain the customer a benefit or prevent a loss, such as with limited time offers, or no-tax sales.

Your price could take a back seat when comparing a competitor's offering. At one point, I offered a barbecue burner for $1.50 more than The Home Depot, but mine was Original Equipment from the Manufacturer (OEM) and The Home Depot's was a generic brand that required some assembly to get it to work.

Consider reference pricing: We are all great at justifying the price we pay when we have some everyday item to reference against. Think about rent versus mortgage payments, or gasoline versus bottled water.

(See a longer description of gain-loss framing in Chapter 7, section 5.)

6. The Power of Ten

In my hardware business, I sold products on a repeat basis to repeat customers. My friend Cal pointed out that customers only recalled the prices of perhaps ten items at most. These ten items are the ones about which the customers demonstrated some price sensitivity. However, my ten items are different from customer Bob's ten items and different again from customer Jerry's ten items.

How could I use this insight? I bought and implemented point of sale software that allowed me to charge different prices to different regular customers. So Bob, who needed a price of $60 to buy a case of lightbulbs, got that price. Jerry paid $66 because lightbulbs weren't one of his price-sensitive items. I made up my desired profit by increasing the prices on items they each bought but where they exhibited no price sensitivity. The customers got the prices they felt were right.

Of course, this applies to the regular business-to-business buyer and not to casual buyers such as those who browse online. Some big online retailers have found a way to implement a means of distinguishing between casual browsers and potential customers (see Chapter 9, section 5. on Dynamic Pricing). Prices increase if you leave and then come back to the site.

7. Paint a Picture in Vivid Primary Colors

Do you recall some purchases more than others? Was it because of the price you paid? Or because the purchase resonated in some manner and you found it easy to sell your spouse or boss on spending that money?

In the 1980s, I worked with the largest distributor of appliances in Western Canada. The company had just become the authorized dealer for Maytag washing machines. Maytag sent along its trainer.

All washing machines look similar; they are often a white metal box with a lid and a control panel. Maytag sold washers on the claim they were "heavy duty."

The Maytag trainer was a large man and he arrived to train the sales staff at 8:00 a.m. Everyone gathered with coffee in hand to listen to him drone on and on about heavy duty springs, special alloys, motors, and belts. As everyone's eyelids began to droop, the trainer placed a step-stool at the side of the washer, opened the lid, and stepped inside. Now he had everyone's attention, and he proclaimed while waving his arms, "THIS ... is heavy duty."

We sold many expensive Maytag washers thanks to this demonstration.

8. Make the Customer Open, If You Can

You as the supplier will have the edge if you can get the potential customer to reveal what he or she thinks will be the right price. Questions such as, "What are you paying now?"; "What did you think it might cost?"; "What is your budget?" are all great ways to get information on the table.

Remember, though, that just dropping a price to meet a budget number is fatal to profits. Remove some value if you are dropping prices.

How? Let's assume that you have qualified the customer for his or her spending budget. No point in test driving new BMWs if the budget is $2,000, right?

The challenge in your business, whether you are a retailer, contractor, service provider, or distributor is to find that real value and shove it into the full glare of the sun to be examined and appreciated by the customer.

So, assume you have established that the budget is $2,000. You can proceed to offer the items at that price point. About now, your sales experience should be kicking in and you have, in your mind, carefully marshaled all the features and benefits that the customer will enjoy if he or she buys this product or service.

First, a terrific item with 16 wonderful features at $1,999. You list each feature, its advantage, and the benefits to the buyer, if he or she buys it. Only at the end when the list is exhausted is price mentioned.

If the buyer does not reach for his or her wallet, then you move down one step to the next item with four benefits stripped away — yes, you must mention that these features are now gone — but now the item costs only $1,600. At this price point, the margins should be the fattest, where you should sell the most and what you inventory the most.

If there is no response from the customer, you present a third choice, of an item with ten benefits removed which undoubtedly means the customer has to do more of the work personally, but now it costs only $999. This is your "save the sale" price point.

The quest in a contracting business should be to build a good customer list, learn to identify the bad customers, and not work yourself to death making quotes for people you should not be entertaining. The axiom is that bad customers drive out good customers because they consume all of your time and resources and force you to ignore the quiet but appreciative customer who is standing there with checkbook in hand. Bad customers demand your time over trivia, are slow to decide, change their requirements midstream, and after all that, are slow to pay.

This entails homework beforehand. A little research can yield whether or not the customer is genuine or just shopping around. More inquiries — "What happened to your last contractor?" — will yield whether they are unreasonable, picky, or a customer that sees value. Pay attention to any complaints about past providers. These are definitely the value indicators that you will need to have in your package for you to succeed (meaning if you want the sale, stress to the customers how you'll avoid whatever problems they previously had).

> **Contractor:** What happened to the last company or person doing the concrete work?
>
> **Customer:** That company was useless. They were always late. The job was late. Then those crooks used substandard concrete. I lost money on the job.
>
> **Contractor:** So in my bid, we can put in a penalty clause if we are late. Would that make you less worried?
>
> **Customer:** I guess so, but what about the concrete?
>
> **Contractor:** If we provided you with documents from the plant showing the quality parameters you ordered and we provided, would that make your engineers happy?
>
> **Customer:** Yeah, it would. Let's discuss this penalty clause …

Notice in the above exchange that the bid is still under consideration. Learning what the customer wants and his or her red button pressure points is just as important here as the price.

9. Make the Buyer Work Hard

At any objection, ask the buyer why (figure out why it's important). Make the buyer justify any objection so that you are uncovering information to help you with the final price. Price objections are not usually a no; rather they are a request for further information.

10. Sandwich Your Price between the Benefits

Whether in person or in writing, the price should come between the first list of benefits and the last list of benefits, and only after you have clearly articulated the benefits of a buying decision.

An example would be "This coat is stylish, the color you like, functional, and the only one you have found today that fits you. The price is $80 and we can put that on your MasterCard so that you have 30 days before you have to pay for it."

Or, "This software package performs all of the functions you have asked for, plus there are added features that are available to use as you get familiar with it. The price is $239 and it comes with easy installation instructions and six months of free support."

11. Try to Make Your Price Nonnegotiable

Don't give any indications early on in the sales discussions that there might be price flexibility. If tested, say that it is very unlikely that prices can be different than quoted.

12. The Cost Penalties of Not Buying

Keep track of the benefits of the product or service you are offering as the benefits become apparent. Place a dollar value on them if possible. "So it takes your shipper six hours to do that job and our service would save four of those hours? At $15 per hour that is $60 in one week and over 50 weeks that would be $3,000, right?" Adding up the benefits at the end puts a dollar value penalty on not buying from you.

13. Don't Squeeze Too Hard Against the Weaknesses

Pigs get fat. Hogs get slaughtered. In other words, don't be greedy or you become the meal. You may wish to have a repeat customer or a referral. If you have the customer at a point of weakness, taking full advantage of that will leave a nasty taste in his or her mouth.

14. Let the Customer Win Something

So you fight over the price and win. Now is the time to make a friend and not an enemy. Let the customer win something small you have saved for the end. But don't just give it away. Let the customer fight for it and then lose gracefully.

15. Laugh Your Way to Your DREAM Price

It is my experience after 13 years in the hardware business that laughing customers don't negotiate well.

When we had an influx of new immigrants to our area we found that, to many of them, the price tag meant nothing and that all prices were supposed to be negotiated. This was a cultural difference with which we struggled for a long while. At least, until I overheard my partsman

Quincy telling a customer holding a small motor that the real price was $4,250 but that today he would be given a special deal of $42.50 (the price on the tag).

16. Don't Email

The research is clear: A face-to-face price presentation is 34 times more successful than an email or a text (Vanessa K. Bohns, *Harvard Business Review*, April 11, 2017). We can read body language in person but not in an email, which begs the question, why do we persist in conducting our primary price negotiations by email instead of face-to-face or at the very least, on the end of the phone?

17. Price in Ranges

If you must negotiate a price for a big client order, is it better to offer a single initial figure or a range? According to a recent study, ranges are the better option.

In other words, open with a price of $7,000 for your car, and you'll get counter-offered $6,500. Open the bidding with a range of $7,000 to $7,500, and the bidding starts at $7,000 (*Profit Report*, Kristine Quan and David Fielding, April 15, 2015).

18. Be Persistent

In Lee Iacocca's book *Iacocca: an Autobiography* on his days in the Ford Lincoln division, he tells the story of honoring the year's top salesman for the division. The fellow called to the podium from the hundreds of car salesmen present was not the sleek, well-groomed, and confident person everyone expected. Instead he was a weedy, bespectacled, and unimpressive man who spoke with a weak and unconfident voice. When asked how he became the company's top salesman, he responded that he just used the sales book as he had been trained, opening it at page one. After going through the features of the car, he would, as per his sales training, then ask the customer if he or she wanted to buy. If no, he or she would go to page two. At the end of page two he would ask the customer if he wanted to buy. If no, then he went to page three. At this point, Iacocca got impatient and asked what happened if he got to the last page and the customer said no for the final time. "Then, Mr. Iacocca, I return to page one and start again."

I have always used this story to illustrate the value of persistence. The story also has value because developing a script ensures that none of the benefits and features of a product are missed (you don't know what is important to a customer). Moreover, the benefits can be expressed in the most positive way. To describe a car as having good tires is mediocre. To say that the car is equipped with top-of-the-line Michelin all-weather radials, while showing the customer the Michelin picture of a baby sitting inside a tire, uses the Michelin brand image to create a fuller picture of the benefits the customer is buying in considering the car you have for sale.

This chapter has presented quite a list and it may not even be exhaustive. If you can master even three of the guidelines you will have an easier time than the average salesperson in getting your dream price. Use Worksheet 1 for practice.

Worksheet 1
Sell Your Price: A Guide for Salespeople

Describe how you will respond to typical questions from customers.

"The price seems high. Why does it cost so much?"

"Is there a discount?"

"When are you having a sale?"

"How do your prices compare to your competitors?"

"Someone else must be cheaper."

Chapter 3
Pricing for Start-ups (and Beyond)

When you are starting a business, you will want to know the key to successfully pricing your product or service on day one. (This chapter will help you if you're just starting out, but if established, read it anyway to see where you stand.)

The most difficult question faced by entrepreneurs is how much to charge for their product or service when they have no history on which to base their numbers. When you are an employee and you respond to a customer with the price, you don't own that price. But as the owner, that question is a gut punch because you know that your customer is thinking that your price is too high!

Typically, people follow the crowd and charge what everyone else charges. This is easy, but also a trap because it leads only to mediocrity.

In a start-up you know everything about the supply: costs, delivery times, conditions. However, you know nothing about demand. Here is my multilayered approach to finding that demand and corresponding prices that generate profits, in the following sections.

1. Provide What the Market Wants; Don't Start by Finding a Market after You Have Made the Product

Most entrepreneurs have a product or service which they love and believe that everyone will buy. Then they start the tedious hunt for customers.

Let us consider a lesson to be learned from Ford and General Motors. In the 1950s General Motors decided to build a sports car to compete with the European sports cars that were entering the market, so the brass went to the engineering department first. The engineers were told to design a sports car. They did and produced a vehicle based on some common GM platforms such as the Bel Air frame but with added refinements for appearances and performance. They built an engineer's car! At the end of the process, the costs were put on the table and a factor added for profit and hey, presto, there was the sale price at $3,450. It didn't sell well because it was considered too expensive. (At one point even the Corvette sold a mere 700 units in a year, but it was saved from the axe by some enthusiastic and devoted engineers.)

In 1960 or thereabouts, Ford conceived the idea of having a sports car also. Lee Iacocca went first to the marketing department and asked them what features and what price was needed in order to sell lots of cars. The research engine got into gear and cranked out a number: $2,500. Iacocca then took this number to engineering and gave them a list of specifications that included the price tag. They fought back about getting the costs that low, but ultimately, 2 inches longer, 200 pounds heavier, built on a Falcon frame, festooned with common Ford components and eight months behind schedule, they produced a car for a selling price of $2,500. The millionth Mustang sold after 13 months and it is still highly regarded as a marketing success story.

While most of us try to figure out the price and where the customers are after we have built the product, the lesson to be learned from this is to find your market first, know what they will buy, how many, and at what price. (See Figure 3.)

2. Customer-Driven Pricing

Should a company owner ask the customer what he or she wants to pay for the product or service on offer and then sell it at that price?

Suppose your nifty new invention solves a problem that plagues most small companies. Should you decide to take this magic widget to the market and ask customers what they will pay for the widget you will

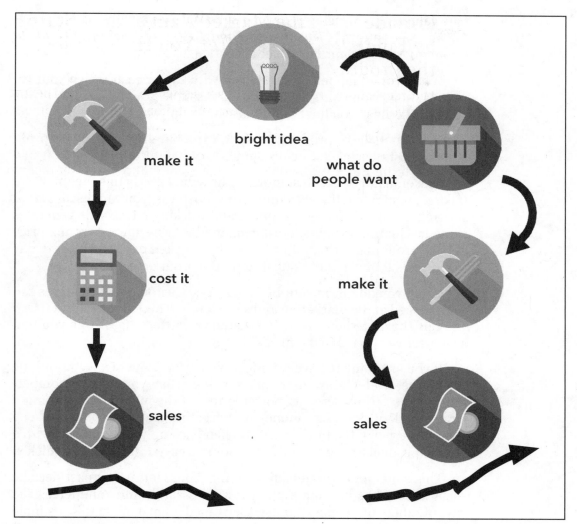

Figure 3: From Idea to Sales

likely get a wide variety of answers from zero to hundreds. After all, the customer has never seen anything like it before.

You are not selling the widget; rather you are selling the solution to the customer's problem. If the problem your widget promises to fix costs hundreds of dollars every year in frustration, downtime, and lost productivity, then the widget will sell for a multiple of that number regardless of what that cost ends up being.

"The job of sales and marketing is not simply to process orders at whatever price customers are currently willing to pay, but rather to raise customers' willingness to pay to a level that better reflects the product's true value ... Low pricing is never a substitute for an adequate marketing and sales effort." (*The Strategy and Tactics of Pricing: A Guide to Growing More Profitably* 4th ed., Routledge, 2005).

What would happen if you started with the price at which your research shows you can sell Product X? Assume you are certain of the volumes because you have a purchase order in your hands.

Can you make or produce Product X for that price and have a profit after all costs are taken into account?

One of history's greatest industrialists did exactly this. Again, we're talking about Ford. If you examine your business, you can discover that starting at the desired end product and working backwards generates some fascinating insights. Ford explained that he started from a price derived from marketing information and worked backwards every day to cut costs to make the product fulfill the profit objective.

Could you do this in your business? Yes. Customer expectations can be managed at the marketing and sales levels. This drives volumes. Can you buy the ingredients or raw materials at better prices? Can you find a smarter way to make the finished product?

If you are going to have pricing driven by customer expectations, be the market leader. Have more market share than your closest competitor. Sell at 7 to 10 percent above the rest of the market and commit a large chunk of that extra money to marketing and advertising to keep you on the top of the brand wagon. Then back up your promises with a quality product and great service. It sounds easy ... if you say it quickly.

This statement will quickly date this book, but in the past decade, social media has become a mainstay of research into commerce. The vast numbers of people who use social media have made this a simple place to test ideas, theories, ask questions, and test pricing — and all for free. Linked with consumer survey companies that exploit this resource, entrepreneurs now have a resource simply not available to previous generations.

Initially, guesswork is all you have for your start-up, so support it with as much primary research as possible. Successful business plans are accompanied by executed contracts, letters of support, or extensive survey results supporting the price and volume considerations.

3. It Is Not about Sales, It Is about Profits

There are three reasons to go into business. First, of course, is to pay yourself better than a living wage. The second is profit. The third is to build wealth.

Notice that sales targets are not included here? Sales are the tool to create the three payoffs. Buying the market by promoting lowball prices does not build wealth, it lowers your profit and has an impact on your take-home pay. Worse, low prices tell everyone that you are a low-quality provider.

If you design your business just to make profit, you will succeed. You can't eat sales, but you can eat profits.

> From 2001 to 2006, The Home Depot grew vigorously and chaotically to become the second-largest retailer in America. Overall, corporate sales grew. Individual store sales lagged. Productivity fell. Profits started to suffer. Comparable store sales at The Home Depot increased an average of 1.4 percent per year, versus an increase of 4.6 percent at Lowe's. As a result, earnings at Lowe's over this period grew at nearly double the rate the Home Depot's did, and Lowe's stock price also doubled, while The Home Depot's stayed flat. The lesson: Growth without profit doesn't work even when you are huge and trying to buy market share.

4. Customer Loyalty and Its Role in Your Pricing

In a study reported at RightNow Technologies (Bob Thompson, "The Loyalty Connection: Secrets to Customer Retention and Increased Profits," magellan-solutions.com/wp-content/uploads/2014/09/Secrets toCustomerRetentionandIncreasedProfits.pdf, accessed March, 2019) the author examined why customers leave and don't come back. His research suggests that the perception of why customers leave is different for customers as opposed to business owners.

In his analysis, customers stopped buying almost 74 percent of the time due to customer service problems while business owners saw customer service as being a reason they lost customers only in 22 percent of the cases. (See Figure 4.)

The same question was asked about quality of the product or service. Quality was seen by customers as the problem 32 percent of the time while owners ranked quality as the issue only 18 percent of the time. (See Figure 5.)

It appears that staff indifference does greater damage to your business than doing a bad job. In other words, the most effective way to drive customers away is to ignore their needs, turn a deaf ear to their complaints, and treat them with indifference or as pests to be swatted.

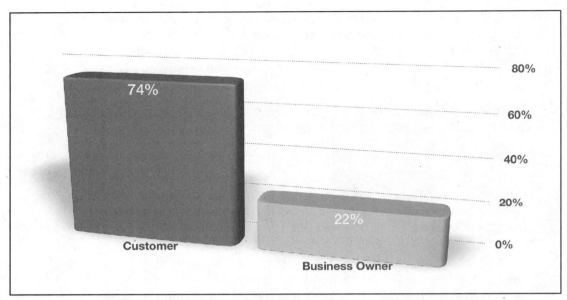

Figure 4: Business Owners Who Think Customers Left Because of Substandard Customer Service

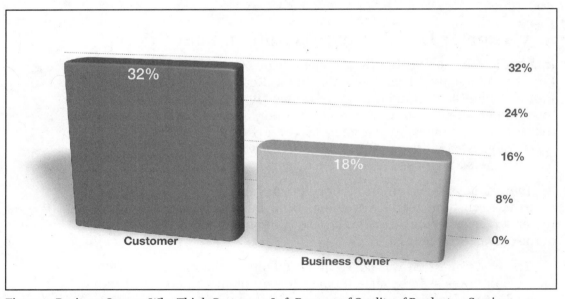

Figure 5: Business Owners Who Think Customers Left Because of Quality of Product or Service

What about price? Pricing was ranked by business owners as the number one cause of losing customers at 36 percent, while customers said they left because of price only 25 percent of the time. (See Figure 6.)

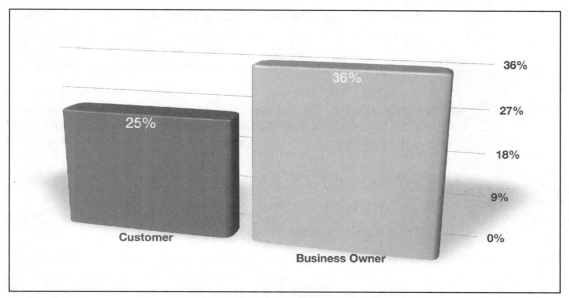

Figure 6: Business Owners Who Think Customers Left Because Price Is Too High

An intriguing indicator is that 35 percent of the time customers claimed the reason they left was that their needs changed, while business owners saw that as being relevant only 8 percent of the time. Perhaps businesses get out of touch with their own customer base and should be regularly contacting their existing customers.(See Figure 7.)

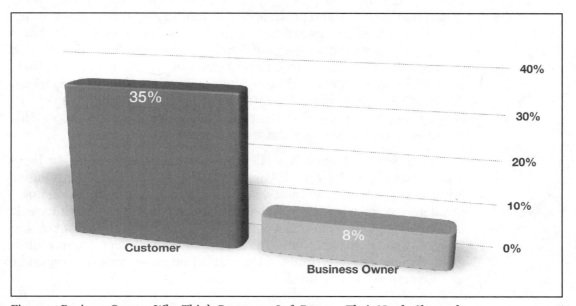

Figure 7: Business Owners Who Think Customers Left Because Their Needs Changed

The consensus among marketers is that consumer demands and needs often escalate in unpredictable ways and trying to read the crystal ball does not work well. It is better to be nimble and react quickly to developing trends. This means constant contact with the customers.

Training your staff to do an outstanding job and your customer response team to treat customers with dignity should be the number one priority. Be brave in your pricing and offer value for money. Work hard to develop a reputation for high quality.

5. Choice and Niche Markets: A Profit Opportunity

There are profit opportunities outside the mainstream.

In a Ted talk a few years ago (www.ted.com/talks/lang/eng/malcolm_ gladwell_on_spaghetti_sauce.html, accessed March, 2019), *The Tipping Point* (Back Bay Books, 2002) author Malcolm Gladwell spoke about the role of choice in buying decisions. When discussing pasta sauce, a manufacturer wanted originally to know what the customer wanted. From that information it would craft a product to fit the customer's taste. Was the customer demanding chunky, spicy, or smooth pasta sauce? Market research came back with a carefully built statistical analysis showing that most people wanted smooth.

By offering only smooth pasta sauce, however, they would have missed niche markets looking for chunky and spicy, with a subsequent loss of market share and profit opportunities in pasta sauces. Some customers on the periphery of the statistical analysis wanted chunky, some spicy, and some even wanted mushrooms. The manufacturer extended its range from 1 sauce to 16 different types of pasta sauce, giving them access to new markets and more shelf exposure in the supermarkets. So the statistical answer was correct but by itself, would have led to a single sauce on the shelf. They needed to see the opportunities outside the mainstream idea to get those extra profits.

When you look at coffee sales, you get the same results. In focus groups, some people will tell you that they like bold coffee with lots of body. Others like lighter roasts, and yet others like it milky. A homogenized market survey will show that statistically most people drink weak, milky coffee. Again, making a coffee for the mainstream market means foregoing some market share. Taking the statistically significant middle ground means that portions of the market on either side of the middle are not served by your product or service.

For a start-up this means look at the fringes and edges for the profit opportunities and not necessarily just the middle of the road where you could be run over.

6. Price in Threes (a.k.a., Good, Better, Best Pricing)

First, you need a dream price. Start your sales offering with the package offering the largest number of features and benefits to the customer — your dream package with its corresponding dream price tag. This is your homegrown reference price to establish in the customer's mind that you offer great service and great products, and they cost.

You need a "value for the money" price. If the dream package is refused because of a thinner wallet, you can offer a lesser package at a price that may fit their budget better. We can do it for that price, what would you like us to leave out?

You are not discounting here, but you are removing features that cost you money while still offering value for money to the customers. This offering is cheaper to provide and hence commands a lower price. The margins remain the same because you are pricing for profit.

Finally, you need a "save-the-sale" price. This is the same product or service but with even more features removed, making it still cheaper to provide and hence commanding an even lower price.

DREAM PACKAGE	16 features/benefits	$3,000
VALUE FOR MONEY	12 features/benefits	$2,500
SAVE THE SALE	10 features/benefits	$1,750

This is also called "Good, Better, Best" pricing and is rampant in industry for a good reason: It works. Consider the sellers of car batteries for example that offer the same battery but for different prices as distinguished by the increasing length of the warranty offered.

Delivery companies offer the same delivery service at different rates depending on how quickly the package must arrive.

Consider that TV networks sell 85 percent of their advertising air time in advance but leave 15 percent open for last-minute, premium customers to buy.

Southwest Airlines (*Nuts! Southwest Airlines' Crazy Recipe for Business and Personal Success*; Crown Business, 1998) created a Business Select Package that sold for a premium price. The airline offered high appeal (but low cost) advantages to the buyer such as priority boarding, extra frequent flier miles, and free cocktails; this all delivered $73 million in increased revenues in the first 12 months.

See Worksheets 2 and 3.

7. Decision Fatigue: Analysis Paralysis and Its Role in Pricing

It is conventional Western wisdom that more choice equals more freedom. But too much choice can lead to paralysis, no decision, or the customer left with a feeling of discontent that with all that choice he or she could have bought something even better.

Researchers set up a jam-tasting stall in a posh supermarket in California. Sometimes they offered 6 varieties of jam, at other times 24. Jam tasters were then offered a voucher to buy jam at a discount.

While more choice attracted more customers to look, very few of them actually bought jam. The display that offered less choice made many more sales; in fact, only 3 percent of jam tasters at the 24-flavor stand used their discount voucher, versus 30 percent at the 6-flavor stand. (*The Paradox of Choice: Why More Is Less*, EccoPress, 2016).

On February 2, 2013, the CBC aired an episode of Terry O'Reilly's program, "Under the Influence." The theme was choice and about how a customer makes a decision when a marketer gets a product in front of him or her. Do you buy or not?

Given too many choices of products or services a customer will simply NOT make a decision and walk away. We are, in this modern world, bombarded by radio, TV, junk mail, and spam to make a decision and buy something. Instinctively we tune out rather than make a bad decision. This is because, according to Terry O'Reilly, we, as humans, have an innate ability to make a fixed number of great decisions per day. After that, decision fatigue sets in and bad choices are made. The example he offered was of President Obama who had only two colors of suits to choose from in his wardrobe: blue and charcoal. Why waste energy on something so insignificant when America's deep financial crisis awaited him?

The lesson to be learned is sometimes you might want to limit choices, particularly of product or service offerings, so as to not overwhelm the customer. There are significant parallels with how the same process of making a choice works in the pricing world as well. Too many price choices will kill a sale.

Worksheet 2
Finding the Minimum Viable Price

There is a price below which you cannot go because you will just not be able to cover your bills. Do you know that number? That number is necessary in analysing your pricing strategy and especially in creating your price points.

Invoice cost of your product or service (what you must cut a check for)	$
Add freight, tax, brokerage	$
Add burden (rent, staff and owner wages, utilities)	$
Add payroll taxes, fuel, lease payments	$
Total	$

DO NOT ADD PROFIT

Your number could be expressed in dollars per hour or dollars per unit or even dollars per square foot in retail sales.

You could also call this your breakeven point.

Average Sales Unit (in dollars) for your business	
Average Direct Costs for your business (related to the average sale unit)	
Fixed expenses on average per month	
Breakeven Point per month: fixed expenses / average sales unit + average direct costs	

Worksheet 3
Develop Your Three Prices

Start by calculating your minimum price: At what price will it make no sense to remain in business?

Establish what will be the starting point – a dream price at which you would really like to sell all the time.

You will need three prices for each category of product or service in order to sell more and maximize your profits. Naturally, your "save the sale" price is well above your minimum viable price.

Then assemble features, advantages, and benefits for each category.

The following table will help:

Feature	Advantage	Benefit
If the feature of a repair center is that you have 10,000 SKUs	Then the advantage is that you are likely to have the part when needed	And the benefit to the customer is the speed of a repair
If the feature of a janitorial company is the use of non-allergenic cleaning products	Then the advantage is that fewer clients will get sick because of the janitors	And the customer will have fewer sick days being taken
If the feature of the company is that it was formed in 1989	Then the advantage is that they are not fly-by-night	And the company will be around to solve problems that may arise

List the features and benefits below, starting with the dream price and then moving to the everyday and "save the sale" prices by stripping out features and benefits that add to your costs. The everyday price is lower than the dream price and the "save the sale" price is lower than the everyday price.

DREAM PRICE = $ _____		
	FEATURE	BENEFIT
1		
2		
3		
4		
5		
6		

Worksheet 3 — Continued

7		
8		
9		
10		
11		
12		

Strip out features and benefits that add to your costs.

EVERYDAY PRICE = $ _____		
	FEATURE	BENEFIT
1		
2		
3		
4		
5		
6		
7		
8		

Strip out features and benefits that add to your costs.

SAVE THE SALE PRICE = $ _____		
	FEATURE	BENEFIT
1		
2		
3		
4		

In my observation with clients and in my own research, offering too many price points on your product or service leads to decision overload. When one of our clients, a hearing aid provider, provided his customers with 14 different price points on similar products, sales stagnated. The customer walked away rather than make a decision.

To solve the problem, we reduced the list to four prices and sales improved.

Why four prices? A single price is a "take it or leave it" ultimatum. No one is comfortable with that and it is simple to say no. Two choices are still a bit black and white. Having three choices appeals to our very human need to be in control, to make an informed decision that can be explained simply thereafter to a spouse or business partner. Moreover, the three choices could be framed as "good, better, best." The fourth choice was a price determined by a government contract.

Done correctly, most customers will choose the middle item or service. This is called the Goldilocks principle. Conventional wisdom makes us suspicious of the lowest price. We have a tougher time justifying a high price unless it is a luxury or occasion-based item such as champagne. The easiest choice should be the middle price. In order to improve profits with my consulting client we deliberately offered the middle product with the highest percentage gross margin. The value-for-money product had a combination of useful but not too elaborate features. The middle offering was qualitatively better than the simple save-the-sale model. The middle product was priced closer to the high end model rather than the save-the-sale model. See Figure 8.

Since most people equate quality with higher prices, we strategically placed the middle product to be an easy consumer choice.

By the way, it was also the most heavily inventoried product.

8. Bad Customers Drive out Good Customers

Time is valuable, so why waste it on customers who don't respect you?

If you have been in business more than five minutes, you will know that there are saints and sinners among your customers. You may be vaguely aware that the sinners take up more of your time than all the saints combined.

There is nothing worse for your firm's morale than to continue to serve customers who do not understand or appreciate the value you provide. Given a choice between continuing a relationship with a toxic

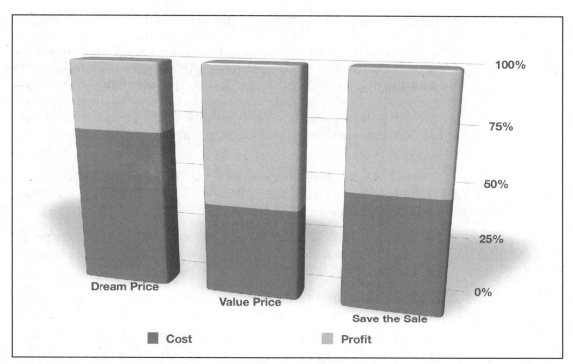

Figure 8: Three Price Packages Expressed as Percentages of Sales

customer and the effect it will have on the morale of your team members, observe who former CEO of Southwest Airlines, Herb Kelleher, sided with, as this story from *Nuts! Southwest Airlines' Crazy Recipe for Business and Personal Success* (Crown Business, 1998) humorously illustrates:

" ... (a) woman who frequently flew on Southwest, but was disappointed with every aspect of the company's operation. In fact, she became known as the Pen Pal because after every flight she wrote in with a complaint. It was quickly becoming a volume until they bumped it up to Herb (Kelleher)'s desk, with a note: 'This one's yours.' In sixty seconds, Kelleher wrote back and said, 'Dear Mrs. Crabapple. We will miss you. Love, Herb.'"

The squeaky wheel gets the grease and difficult customers get the attention of management. This is normal and to expect that all things will happen quietly and profitably is unrealistic. Successful businesses spend time and effort on their good customers and don't take them for granted.

9. Wrapping It All Together

Pricing is tough to get right especially in the first year of operations. For a start-up to price its product or service profitably and therefore grow takes hard work. Certainly it is harder work than merely copying the price of your competitors. But some steps to rationalize the process will pay dividends because it is simple to make fine adjustments to a well thought out pricing strategy than design a new one each time you hit a bump in the road.

Do your market research and find out before you open the doors what people want and what they will pay. Direct your efforts to marketing and offering what people want.

Offer what people will pay for and structure your efforts for profit, not just sales. Offer quality, outstanding customer service because this is what customers want.

Find the niche markets where the big companies do not compete well and consider becoming good at selling those products or services.

Offer choice, just not too much choice. Three price options are optimal; each reflecting decreasing/increasing value for money. When you have to drop from the dream package price down to the next level, cut out value and not profits.

Pay attention to attracting and retaining quality customers. Start-ups invariably attract awful customers because no one else will deal with them anymore.

When you have a solid grasp of these concepts, get out there and sell at your dream price.

Chapter 4
Positioning for Price (The Role of the Unique Selling Proposition)

The purpose of this chapter is to make your Unique Selling Proposition (USP) into a principal aspect of your pricing strategy. Knowing how to define, understand, and utilize this vital concept is an important step in knowing how to improve your prices. After all, if your business is one white sheep in a herd of white sheep then you will compete only on price and prices will inevitably grind down to the lowest possible dollar. When you have some value to offer and can define that to stand head and shoulders about the crowd, your company can become the price leader instead of the price follower.

A study, repeated in different ways in many parts of the world, shows that high price is associated in the consumer's mind with high quality, particularly for product groups involving fashion or taste. Why else would perfumes, diamonds, and champagne sell for such high prices?

1. How Do You Use a Unique Selling Proposition?

When using a USP, keep in mind:

- Each advertisement must make a proposition to the customer: "Buy this product, and you will get this specific benefit."

- The proposition itself must be unique; something that competitors do not, or will not, offer.

- The proposition must be strong enough to pull new customers to the product.
- I would add that the USP must answer the question: "What's in it for me?"

Some good current examples of products with a clear USP are:

Head & Shoulders: "You get rid of dandruff."

Olay: "You get younger-looking skin."

Some unique propositions that were pioneers when they were introduced:

Domino's Pizza: "You get fresh, hot pizza delivered to your door in 30 minutes or less, or it's free."

FedEx: "Your package absolutely, positively has to get there overnight."

M&M's: "The milk chocolate melts in your mouth, not in your hand."

Wonder Bread: "It helps build strong bones 12 ways."

How can the small business owner apply this axiom and turn it alchemically into cash?

In the next sections I delineate nine steps to position for price.

2. Step 1: Dissect Why You Originally Decided to Sell Your Widgets or Services

Take one widget or job that your company offers and ask yourself what the original concept in selling this was?

Was it because no one offered this product or service? Perhaps someone else offered it badly? What makes your product or service better than the others? What makes your company different? Are you just one of many?

If all you can think of is "we have better service," then you are in the pricing game only.

Even in the so-called commodity markets where price is supposed to be the only determiner of where business is placed, a USP differentiates the providers. Consider the buyers in the auto industry who buy sheet steel using exceedingly tight technical specifications. They demand much more than the steel itself. They also demand certain delivery conditions and flexibilities, price and payment conditions, and reordering responsiveness. From year to year, the auto manufacturers shift the proportions of steel they buy from their various suppliers on the basis of elaborate grading systems that measure each supplier's performance on the specified conditions, including the kind and quality of unsolicited help on such matters as new material ideas, ideas for parts redesign, and even purchasing procedures.

If you are offering the same product as everyone else — snowmobiles from Yamaha, smartphones from Samsung, or roofing tiles from DuPont — you can still find ways to differentiate the way the company delivers the undifferentiated goods. Do you offer something the competition cannot offer? Do you offer service in the home? Or on Saturdays?

This must be your *Star Trek* moment, to go where nobody has gone before or even dares to go.

There is the case of the "Bugs" Burger Bug Killer Company (based in Miami, Florida, then run by Al Burger), a pest control company specializing in the hospitality industry. Al knew most companies did not want to control pests, but to wipe them out, so he developed an extraordinary guarantee to convince his customers that he could do the job. This is his powerful guarantee.

THE B.B.B.K. GUARANTEE

GUARANTEED PERFORMANCE

1. You do not pay our initial charges until we Totally Eliminate every roach, rat or mouse nesting on your premises.

2. If you are ever dissatisfied with our results and want to cancel our service due to a re-infestation of roaches, rats or mice, we will:

   A. Refund up to one year's service charge and...
   B. Pay the cost of another exterminator of your choice for up to one year.

3. Should a roach or rodent be seen by one of your guests, we will PAY THEIR BILL,* send them a letter of apology and invite them back as our guest.

"BUGS" BURGER BUG KILLERS, INC.
The Original Pest Elimination Company™

Or how about this promise that H&R Block used years ago that adds value and commands the price by reducing risk?

> **"We Take Responsibility for Our Mistakes**
>
> Our associate training and system of safeguards are carefully designed to ensure the accuracy of your return. Mistakes are rare at H&R Block. However, if we do make an error in the preparation of your tax return that costs you any interest or penalty on additional taxes due, we will reimburse you for the interest and penalty."
>
> (www.hrblock.ca/our_company/guarantee.asp, accessed 2008).

What makes you and your company so different that you can justify higher prices? If you were a customer of either of the above companies, wouldn't it make sense to pay their top dollar? Even better, the above guarantee forces the customer to focus on the value proposition of a low-end service provider. Being shut down is the terror of most managers of hotel and restaurants. The costs would be astronomical and the damage to reputation. So the cost of roach control is minor compared to that, right? Why buy cheap for such a critical service?

Being called for an audit by Canada Revenue Agency is a nightmare most of us would pay money to avoid. So why not use the services of H&R with its comforting guarantee?

3. Step 2: Unearth Those Customer Benefits

Figure out what your customer benefits are by mining your sales pitch. Your tried and true sales technique provides the raw material to develop a USP.

In what way can you create a dynamic picture of what makes you different? In the 1960s, Ford's Malibu engineers proclaimed that the car was the smoothest ride in town. "Prove it," the marketers retorted and the engineers did that by placing a bottle of powerful acid over an expensive fur coat in the Malibu while it drove over rough roads. The marketers were so impressed at this visual illustration of the smooth ride that multiple expressions of the same idea were shown in TV advertising for the car.

Figure 9, configured for your business, can become the nucleus of a great selling proposition. (Remember Worksheet 3? Those concepts repeated.)

Unless your customer is an engineer, the latest product specifications, and the features, are gibberish. Converting them to believable benefits for the customer takes practice.

Feature	Advantage	Benefit
If the feature of a repair center is that you have 10,000 SKUs	Then ... the advantage is that you are likely to have the part when needed	And ... the benefit to the customer is the speed of a repair.
If the feature of a janitorial company is the use of non-allergenic cleaning products	Then ... the advantage is that fewer clients will get sick because of the janitors	And ... the customer will have fewer sick days being taken.
If the feature of the company is that it was formed in 1989	Then ... the advantage is that it is not a fly-by-night	And ... the company will be around to solve problems that may arise.

Figure 9: Features, Advantages, and Benefits

You could be selling new drill bits with titanium points. They are harder and can drill longer without sharpening. However, that has to become a tangible benefit by translating from "longer between sharpening" to something like 14 percent more holes drilled. At that point, the potential bulk user will grab the calculator and cost out his downtime for drill changes and then the cost of resharpening. Price has become a secondary issue compared to the cost savings. This is also called "Gain Loss" pricing.

For example, pool noodles: You know those colored foam round sticks that children play with in swimming pools? A number of summers ago, I saw a gas station selling them in a rural area displaying a sign proclaiming their price. The sign said "Cheaper than Canadian Tire in Town." Why, I thought would you advertise like that when you could have posted a sign reading instead "Only $1 more than Canadian Tire, 20 miles away." They were simply giving up bottom line dollars.

4. Step 3: Analyze Your Customer

In analyzing your customer you want the answer to the question, "Why do you buy from me?"

The cost of your product or service may be evaluated by a buyer in terms of the functionality of the offering, the durability, the reliability, the after-market service, freight costs, installation, and payment terms, to name a few considerations.

In your sales offering, have you addressed each of these in a way that means something to the customer? This is the process known as value pricing.

A manufacturing company in a suburb of Vancouver had a short and expressive motto that addressed customer concerns immediately: "Quality on Time." This boast was backed up with data. The company delivered plus or minus one day from the promised date and had a measurable 97 percent acceptance rate at the shipping door. The three words told everyone that the company paid utmost attention to rampant industry problems, which were that people were often receiving subpar orders late.

If this were not the case, then price will become the only determining factor.

You leave money on the table when you don't know what your customer wants and what he or she is prepared to pay for the value you add to your product or service. Often enough the biggest problem facing a re-examination of price structure is that the company has become comfortable in its groove of selling an item at $0.49 when, in fact, there is a chance that it could sell the same quantity for $3.49.

In my hardware store I had a conundrum. We sold lots of four-groove belts and a few of the matching motors. The belts cost $0.99. The motors cost $72, but no one would pay the price I wanted at full margin for the motors. To sell any I had to drop the price to $99 from $129. So I compensated and sold the belts, no longer at $4.99 retail, but $11.00 retail. Sales continued as normal.

I recall when a US firm charged $0.37 for work gloves, they did not sell. When the price was raised to $0.39 the buyers snapped them up.

5. Step 4: Examine the Customer Cost Variables

Before setting price levels, examine the customers' perception of what a cost is.

As an example, in the article "Industrial Pricing to meet customer needs" (*Harvard Business Review*. No.78609. November-December 1978), it said: "One manufacturer of laboratory instruments was plagued by a high number of very small orders for a limited variety of repair parts for one particular product line. On analysis, the product manager found that customers were annoyed at having to order small parts because the ordering cost was greater than the parts prices. Furthermore, the company was losing money on the parts for the same reason.

"Even more costly, customers were upset at the downtime caused by not having the correct parts in stock. A few customers with many instruments seemed capable of keeping the right mix of parts in stock but others with limited experience could not develop good inventory rules. To alleviate the problem, the product manager developed repair kits with several different assortments of parts and offered them to customers using a large variety of instruments. The company's costs went down, customer costs decreased, and customer satisfaction increased because instruments were available more of the time."

If you were the manufacturer of the laboratory instruments, the salesperson's tool bag would need to contain this story to demonstrate the impact that decreasing the amount of instrument downtime had on the customer's ability to perform. Again, this example lends itself well to building a case before price is mentioned in the sales presentation. The downtime is a cost in the eyes of the customer.

I used to sell repair parts for barbecues. One Saturday, a customer came in and asked for a Shepherd bottom burner. I had an Original Equipment Manufacturer (OEM) part and the price was $54 plus tax. The customer hesitated.

So I said to the customer: "You are thinking that it might be cheaper across the road at the big chain hardware store. Right?"

He nodded.

I said, "Well, it is cheaper by $1.50 and it is a universal part that only requires some assembly. "

Panic stole across his face as he recalled the effort to assemble the barbecue in the first place and the resultant argument with his wife.

He bought the burner at my price.

6. Step 5: Use the Power of Ten

Years ago when I owned a hardware store, my friend Cal Swane and I were discussing the myopia of our respective customer bases. It was amusing and disconcerting to us that customers knew the price of perhaps ten items intimately. They knew where the best prices were to be had and when sales happened. For suppliers like us they were a nightmare because they expected us to meet or improve upon those prices they had welded to their foreheads. To drop the price to meet the

Sometimes knowing your market leads to unexpected decisions. In the 1980s we marketed our installation company's services to the supposedly well-to-do part of town. We got the calls and did the work; only to be told that the check would be in the mail or to have their credit cards rejected. The service technicians told me tales of installing top-of-the-line products in houses where the furniture was upturned plastic milk crates.

At the same time, our business in the "working class" part of Vancouver produced no problems. In fact, most often we were paid in cash from a roll of bills produced from a pocket of the homeowner.

The lesson: Part of your target market consideration should be the ability to pay.

expectations of one client meant dropping that price for everyone using standard inventory control software. Worse, there would be an impact on the bottom line since the ten items Fred remembered were neither the same ten items recalled by Joe nor the same ten as memorized by Richard. I tried dropping the price for everyone and lost 13 percent of my margin in one year. Maintaining some sort of handy list to remind us and our staff that a special price was available for chosen clients and then overriding the standard pricing was a clumsy remedy. We tried that too.

Ultimately, I installed software that would allow me to adjust prices for one customer but not another, thereby better maintaining my profit margins.

The real point of the discussion was how a customer, client, or patient feels about your overall pricing based on a few scraps of information. This is where the pricing solution above works well to create an impression of having best prices in town without really dropping prices to dangerous levels.

All of us monitor the price of gasoline and we have all seen in person or on the TV the long lineups of cars trying to get gas before it jumps one cent. Yet we happily pay more for bottled water than for gasoline. So paying attention to what your customers are telling you in discussion or through their buying practices is the route to profit nirvana. You can be viewed as the best buy on the street or the one to avoid. It is your choice.

7. Step 6: Make the Customer's Choice Easy

When I owned an installation company in Vancouver in the 1980s and 1990s, we worked hard to keep prices universal for standard jobs. Our marketing edge — successfully employed to gain an 80 percent market share — was to offer the benefit of a fixed price where none had existed before. Customers bought our services because we gave them a closed-ended transaction.

This is the point of franchises. The benefit of a McDonald's hamburger restaurant is that a Big Mac will consistently taste the same whether you bought it in Vancouver, Boston, or Berlin. The price may vary from country to country but the delivered product does not. Coca-Cola operates in the same way.

Niche market franchisers such as Mr. Lube have created a business out of having a one-price shop. Are there cheaper places to get an oil change? Undoubtedly, but they do not have the marketing and advertising clout to carve out a large share of the available market.

8. Step 7: Exploit Perceived Value

For some years there was a mighty battle between Intel and AMD to dominate the market for processing chips. Intel kept ahead of its competition by being innovative and adding features faster than its competitors. Its Pentium chip took a huge market share until AMD invested heavily and matched the Pentium's performance. That eliminated Intel's pricing advantage. "Recognizing that AMD could quickly match future technological advances made by Intel, management turned their attention from features that drove customer costs and were easy to copy, to features that drove customer revenues and were harder to copy" (*The Strategy and Tactics of Pricing: A Guide to Growing More Profitably*, Routledge, 2005).

Their research showed that customers were more likely to buy a product when they knew what processor was in the box. Hence was born the "Intel Inside" marketing campaign. Intel commanded a premium price for the chip because its advertising drove the sales of the computer manufacturers. AMD could not follow since it was lesser known except to computer geeks.

9. Step 8: Who and When Is Your Customer?

A common mistake made by pricing managers is to assume that their objective is to set a price for the product rather than the customer segment. (*The Strategy and Tactics of Pricing. A Guide to Growing More Profitably,* Routledge, 2005.)

There are dozens, perhaps hundreds of market segments for your product or service all commanding different price points.

Is your potential customer a millennial, wealthy, tile layer, retired, B2B, or seasonal?

If your business targets seniors, then price can likely be 100 percent of the buying decision.

If your business targets the wealthy, where price is no object, then sale prices make no sense.

Imagine that today you have $80,000 in your pocket and you want to buy a luxury car to impress a lovely lady, but the salesperson keeps showing you economy cars. Will you buy? Is it price that makes the decision for you?

Or, imagine that today you need a car to get you back and forth from work. You have $13,000 and on the car lot is a General Motors product for $12,500, and beside it is a $6,900 car made by some company you have never heard of before. Which will you buy?

As far as timing, as in when you will sell, in my hardware business I sold mostly B2B (Business to Business) and my customers had calendar-year budgets. No pricing or tantalizing offer could tempt them to buy when the budget was exhausted. So we took great advantage of a slow December to recharge and get our inventory up to date for the January rush. It's good to know when your orders are likely to come in.

This is a data-driven world and the more you know about your target market, the more you will be able to profit.

> In the early 1970s a Swedish manufacturer of drilling equipment, supplying the British Columbia market, was unable to supply a simple O-ring. Drilling equipment became idle as this seemingly insignificant part failed. The specific part was expensive if compared to other O-rings, but a microscopic fraction of the cost of a machine being idle at thousands of dollars per hour.
>
> The local sales manager went off in search of an unauthorized local alternative. He presented a Vancouver-based rubber manufacturer with a sample to see if they might have a suitable substitute, only to be asked how many he wanted. Nervously asking if he could have a dozen, the counterman replied that he could have a box of 100 if needed. Afraid that the price would break the bank based on what they paid Sweden, the manager asked the price and was told that the price was literally pennies per ring. The company he had found was the supplier to Sweden.

10. Step 9: Think Like a Customer

Once you have your USP, and you can in 25 words or less articulate what's in it for your customer, it is time to apply the same thinking to your customers. Who in your customer list will respond best to these arguments? Who, in the untouched marketplace will respond positively to being told that your product or service will save them untold thousands in reduced downtime?

What this means is that in trying to convert a potential janitorial company to your line of floor wax stripper, you must first find out the company's hidden costs. In converting will they have to retrain staff? In converting will they have to retrain customers? In converting what will they do with the 450 gallons of floor stripper they currently use that is in their warehouse? In converting, will they have to update sales brochures or other materials?

11. Using Your USP to Position for Price

Why is your USP so powerful? If your company does not stand out in the crowd, then your company is not fulfilling its profit potential. Profit engineering starts with an outstanding USP.

GOOD UNIQUE SELLING PROPOSITION = GREATER PROFITS = HAPPIER CUSTOMERS

Use Worksheet 4 to develop your USP.

Worksheet 4
Develop Your Unique Selling Proposition

Where are you positioning the company? At the top end of the market? Middle or bottom?

What part of the market are you targeting and why?

Are you competing directly with big competitors in the middle of the road? Or are you establishing yourself in a niche market where the competition will hesitate to follow?

How are you helping your customer?

How are you helping your customer to reduce risk or stress?

How are you helping your customer get things done?

How are you removing surprises for your customer?

Express this in 25 vivid words or less.

HINTS:

• If your USP sounds like your competitors', try again. You have not identified why anyone should buy from you.

• If your USP depends on flabby words such as service, friendly, or quality, then try again. These words do not paint a picture.

Chapter 5
Value Pricing

Value, like truth, beauty, and contact lenses, is in the eye of the beholder.

Value pricing is a pricing strategy which sets prices primarily on the value as perceived by the customer and is disconnected from the cost of the product or historical prices.

Building on the development of a great unique selling proposition, you can translate that into profitable pricing using value.

A business owner must see his or her business as a daily battle to create differences between his or her bakery and Billy's bakery across the street. A victory in this battle means that customers will pay the asked price for quality, convenience, or selection. Defeat means that your customers will reduce everything to the simplest comparable state — apples to apples, loaves to loaves — dollars per unit. This is how customers will make a buying decision, by boiling down choices to the simplest common denominator; a situation what will certainly occur if you do not strive to offer value and which will result in you dropping your prices to compete.

Commodities such as flour, pork bellies, and water are traded on the world market on price alone. A successful business should be striving to steer away from stark yes or no decisions and present itself as that highly desirable, nutritious, refreshing, sexy, and distinctive water that will have potential customers oohing and aahing. That is how you get your price.

If your business wants to be successful, then don't put price on the table before you have offered value. In your store or sales presentation, value should be offered first and price last. (Refer back to Chapter 2.) You alone can prevent the customer from taking the easy route and making a comparison on price alone. If you introduce price in the first breath, you have just told the customers that their choice must be on price alone and your efforts to add value after that are all wasted.

So where is the value? What makes your product especially good and a benefit to all who buy it? Is it healthful? Will it save time and money? Is it the best fitting and best looking blouse on the racks today?

If you are selling something wherein everyone knows the price, such as crude copper, what is the value proposition in dealing with your company? Is it the payment terms? Free delivery? Just in time delivery? Do you have acres of parking? What value is buried in the price that you can bring into the sunshine for your customers to say ooh and aah?

Salt is added to wine to create cooking wine and to prevent it being used as a cheap alternative to drinking wine.

1. What Is Value Pricing Exactly?

1.1 Value pricing is champagne

Consider champagne, which is only fizzy white wine after all, typically with higher prices. The makers have kept improving sales in a market for alcohol that is uniformly declining across the developed world by positioning champagne as the special occasion drink. Could you imagine celebrating your tenth wedding anniversary with a bottle of Pepsi? I can imagine divorce lawyers having a giggle over that one.

1.2 Value pricing is DuPont pipe

As stated in "Industrial Pricing to Meet Customer Needs" (*Harvard Business Review*, No.78609. November-December 1978), "In July, 1954, DuPont introduced Alathon 25, a new polyethylene resin used in pipe manufacture. Until that time, all polyethylene pipes had been made from a by-product of off-grade resin. While pipe produced from Alathon 25 looked exactly like pipe made from off-grade resin, it had a longer life than competitive pipe and could withstand greater pressure.

"After the product's shaky entry in to the market, DuPont developed a strong promotional program for Alathon 25 which communicated its notable benefits to a careful selection of the extruders who made the resin into pipe. Alathon 25 sales grew strongly despite the fact that extruders sold the pipe to distributors for between $9.50 and $13.00 per 100 feet versus the $5.00 to $7.00 price for pipe made from off-grade resin. This price ratio, almost 1.9 is greater than the relative lives of the pipe would suggest.

"An advertisement reproduced in the case study shows the secret of this strategy's success. It shows a farm application, a typical use of this pipe, where the pipe goes underground. It is clear that if the pipe bursts, it would have to be dug up — a time consuming, muddy and expensive chore. The value or utility of the pipe is great because it is part of a complex system."

1.3   Value pricing is printing chocolate bar wrappers

In *The Goal II: It's Not Luck* (Productivity & Quality, 2005), the author encounters a printing firm struggling to make sales in a market dominated by competitors with huge, modern printing machines that cranked out chocolate bar wrappers at top speed.

The salespeople complained that the price needed to be lowered to compete. The older, slower machines in use by the company could not be forced to work harder. Was this a dead end?

The consultants noted that the time charged to set up a machine for a print run represented a large sum whether they printed thousands or millions. This of course, affected the final price.

During the investigation stage, one of the consultants got his hands on a trade magazine that stated that the average life expectancy of a chocolate bar wrapper was six months. This meant that every six months the candy manufacturer would change the wrapper in some way to keep the product looking current and updated.

The professional buyers were asking the sales team to quote on a one-year supply. Here was the opening.

The sales team went back to the buyers and asked what happened to the overstock. They are thrown away, said the buyers. So the order could be for a six-month supply and with a short run like that, the company could compete. The bonus was that the company could also offer to deliver three months worth of wrappers at a time, saving cash flow and warehouse space and handling.

1.4   Value pricing is Donald Cooper's clothing store

What about stores that offer benefits aside from a great product at a value price? Donald Cooper described how customers drove 100 miles to visit his clothing store in Guelph, Ontario, because he catered to the emotional needs of the women who shopped there. He used part of the valuable space of his store to offer a crèche for women with children after noting that women accompanied by children would have fewer than ten minutes of time to shop for the right skirt or blouse before the children got bored and demanded to go home. The crèche solved that because the children were occupied and safe and the ladies could shop for as long as they wished. To those ladies, the clothing on the racks was cheap at the price for the quiet personal time Cooper gave them for free.

2. Applying Value Pricing: Pricing on Purpose

You will never get paid more than you think you are worth.

If you have already been convinced that value pricing is worth attempting, then read the following letter first.

"Finally ... the biggest change in all of this has been to my self-esteem. About ten years ago, not long after beginning my solo practice, my mother-in-law, who is an attorney, said to me, 'Diane, just remember, men are in business to make money and women are in business to take care of people. Get over it!' What she meant was that the female attitude of 'I'll take care of you' will give you little satisfaction and make you no money. If you are going to be taken away from your family, you might as well make a hell of lot of money, and feel really good about it. But that is easier said than done. I fell into the trap of helping my clients and forgetting myself. Was I popular? Did my clients love me? Yes! But I didn't feel the same. Only when I took my practice seriously and began placing a value on my services by Pricing on Purpose did I begin to feel successful. If you feel successful, you are successful and then the money follows. When you reduce your value due to an hourly rate it feels lousy, no matter how high the billing rate." (*Pricing on Purpose: Creating and Capturing Value*, John Wiley and Sons Inc., 2006.)

To begin, you must have a handle on your costs. Knowing how to produce the metrics for your company and its products or service is the prerequisite to creating the metrics to answer the questions in Worksheet 5; how you attach a number to some of the answers to these questions. Moreover, you will realize from these questions that the salespeople will have to understand their customer intimately in order to make this process work.

3. Value Pricing Is Tip Pricing

TIP pricing is the acronym for To Insure Performance and can easily be thought of as a tip for exemplary performance. Two decades ago, I worked for a Chicago-based business consultancy. My first exposure to

Worksheet 5
Figure out Your Value

How are we helping our customers to grow their businesses and be more profitable?	
How are we helping our customers to reduce risk?	
How are we making our customers' businesses more valuable?	
How are we helping our customers get things done?	
How are we removing surprises for our customers?	
At what price would our customers not consider buying?	
At what price would our product or service be expensive but our customers still buy it?	
At what price would our product be inexpensive?	
At what price does the pricing become so inexpensive that our customers question its value?	
What price would be the most acceptable?	
At the new target price, can we make a profit above our costs?	
How will we segment the market and offer different prices to different customers?	
How much volume can we afford to lose due to a price increase and still maintain profit levels?	

This chart is modeled after the book *Pricing on Purpose: Creating and Capturing Value* (John Wiley and Sons Inc., 2006) and shows the questions that must be asked to determine the value-added aspects of your product or service.

value-based pricing occurred in the training and I did not, at the time, realize what was happening. Most of the focus of the training period was on gaining familiarity with the tools to analyze a business and pick apart areas of cost and deviations from the norm. So far, that is standard cost accounting methodology.

Then we practiced adding together the costs over a period of years and presenting this as the opportunity cost if the business was as well managed as it could be. This, we all knew, was a sales technique.

Then we came to the question of the fees that would be charged for a program to rectify this situation. At this point, none of the trainers gave a straight answer. "What would you like it to be?" was the response. We were all dumbfounded and spent a few hours in the bar afterwards discussing this cryptic answer. How, after all, could we place a number on the value of a consulting contract from knowing just the financial penalties being paid for not correcting the business?

That is precisely what was required. If the costs over a period of four years had been $180,000, then a fair price could be anywhere from $180,000 (1:1 and a little unlikely) to $1 (1: $180,000, also unrealistic). The consulting packages sold for multiple of the penalties and/or costs. Ultimately, I settled on a formula that was easy to grasp. The savings from implementing the suggested reforms would repay the consulting fee 18 times over.

Of course, you must know the time you expect to spend on this project and the out-of-pocket expenses you will probably incur. Likely, a successful consultant already goes through this process. If the selling price is higher than your expected costs, then you have a profit.

4. Value Pricing Is Tip Pricing: Accounting

TIP clauses in contracts are also referred to as a retrospective price clause, or success pricing. Example: "In the event that we are able to satisfy your needs in a timely and professional manner, you have agreed to review the situation and decide whether, at the sole discretion of XYZ Company, some additional payment to ABC, the consultant, is appropriate in view of your overall satisfaction with the services rendered by ABC."

I paraphrase here at length from *Pricing on Purpose* because it shows an early attempt at value pricing that was a huge success and convinced the accounting company to abandon hourly rates.

In this case study from 2000, Gus Stearns, a partner in an accounting firm told an amazing TIP story. An accounting engagement had already begun with a price tag of $180,000, derived from estimated hours at

$180 per hour. Gus, the accountant, approached the client and re-opened the contract by talking up the value added by the work to be done. The client was invited to consider the value that could be added by a more successful outcome.

The client got excited by the possibility of huge savings and with little prodding offered a million-dollar TIP. Never once in the discussion were hours or time mentioned. Value took front and center in the negotiations.

5. Value Pricing for Distributors

Distributors are typically judged by whether they have the inventory when you need it or whether they are out of stock.

For example, my boss waltzed one of our OEM suppliers through the door of my office to deliver a complaint that we didn't buy enough from his company. In the same breath, the supplier announced that his business had a sale and wouldn't I like to buy some? I checked my sales and inventory levels and then the price. It was attractive enough for me to place an order for several months' worth of inventory, but the goods were never delivered. They were out of stock. My comment to my boss afterwards was that my price was even better when I had no inventory to sell.

6. Pricing for Value

Value pricing works because it incorporates four important aspects of pricing:

1. Convincing your customer that you are performing miracles when you put so much value on the table for them to buy.

2. Being brave and charging what you are worth.

3. Understanding what the customer values.

4. Understanding what your customer is willing and able to pay for the value you offer.

Put together the ideas in this chapter and discover what value you can communicate to your customers.

Chapter 6
Pricing and Branding

We all know companies that charge premium prices for their products. These include household names such as Mercedes, Prada, Louis Vuitton, and Burberry. Which came first, the high prices or the brand?

High prices are universally meant to signal high quality or to demonstrate the prestige of the buyer.

In *The Loyalty Connection* (magellan-solutions.com/wp-content/uploads/2014/09/SecretstoCustomerRetentionandIncreasedProfits.pdf, accessed March, 2019), these claims of high quality have to be justified by customer experience. How else could companies repeatedly sell their overpriced products year after year?

Brand, it seems, is created by, longevity in the marketplace and public recognition that comes about through a strong presence in the media. These companies spend a ton of money telling us that their products are worth every penny. That advertising reinforces a feeling that buying their product is an indicator of great taste or status. From the branding exercise develops the ability to charge premium prices.

Unfortunately, I have worked with companies that had this backwards. They put higher prices before the hard work to create the brand, and sales were difficult to achieve.

How does this impact a business, day to day? Several years ago, I was asked to intervene in a transaction where the two partners were about to part company. The departing partner had a valuation of his shares in the company that was significantly at variance with the value placed on the same shares by the remaining partner.

The valuation was high because the future sales and profits of the company were taken into account. When asked how that method could be justified, the reply was that the brand name and hence future sales justified that.

My response was to ask what would happen if the price of the product doubled overnight? How many customers would stop buying? The answer was that all of the customers would stop buying. My conclusion was that the company had no recognizable brand yet, and to put a value on something that was still embryonic was unfair to the remaining partner. The valuation was simply too high.

In the 1970s, Ford's luxury Lincoln division had a huge problem with quality, as taken from Lee Iacocca's autobiography. Habitual buyers of these upper-end cars were disappointed that the ignition systems came out with the ignition key, that moldings did not fit, that they rattled ... all the Lincoln dealerships were instructed from head office to call customers and ask about their level of satisfaction. Of course, with the quality problems, this generated a tsunami of complaints that had to be remedied as warranty work. A huge tsunami, except at one dealership — and they were reprimanded for not calling the customers. "But, we do," protested the dealership managers. "We call every customer." So why are your complaint rates much lower than the rest of the network? "Well, we don't like the questions you suggest we ask. Instead, when we call, we ask, 'Mr. Smith, how do your neighbors like your brand new Lincoln?'"

The point of this example is that Lincoln could survive a quality crisis because of its image as a luxury brand was sturdy enough. Price and margins remained healthy.

Burberry of London, maker of high-priced and heavily branded overcoats spotted a problem in 2007. Burberry noticed that they were selling too many coats and that their exclusive brand was being diluted. What to do? The company concluded that they needed to re-establish the exclusiveness of the brand and that the easy to do this was to triple their prices. It worked. Sales dropped by 20 percent and Burberry products became exclusive again.

Healthy foods compete against heavily branded, processed fast food. Burger King is demonstrably not Prada and conveys no social status. However, a study showed the impact of branding on consumption and its relationship to pricing.

I am extracting the pertinent information on pricing food, from a learned article by two researchers called "Does Food Marketing Need to Make Us Fat?" (Chandon, Pierre and Brian Wansink, *Nutrition Reviews*, 70:10 [October].)

Most food is still sold as a commodity which has brought with it a steady decline over the past 50 years in the relative cost. We spend less on food as a proportion of our income, certainly in North America, than previously. But does price or discounting influence purchasing?

The authors pursued a number of studies on the effect of price on purchase decisions that are important for the savvy businessperson.

The average price elasticity of food consumption is low. We need to eat to survive! But, long-term, low retail prices for food, especially fast food, have resulted in people consuming more, as measured in the increasing rates of obesity.

Higher prices can lead to reduced consumption. A 10 percent increase in the price of fast food leads to a statistically correlative reduction in obesity of 0.7 percent.

Pricing is a stronger motivator in a buying decision than nutritional labeling, a strategy that sometimes backfires because nutritional labeling is often associated with no flavor or awful taste.

"The only exception to the rule that higher prices reduce consumption comes from a study showing that higher prices at an all-you-can-eat pizza restaurant led to higher consumption of pizza, probably because of the psychology of 'sunk costs,' which leads people to try to eat their money's worth."

In the short term, significant price reductions can lead to measurable increases in consumption.

Probably the best evidence of this comes from a randomized controlled field experiment involving 1,104 shoppers. This study found that a 12.5 percent temporary price discount on healthier foods increased the purchase volume of these foods by 11 percent among the low-income consumers who received the coupons. The effect persisted even six months after the promotion had been stopped.

This is important because low-income shoppers mind their pennies and are motivated to buy as many calories per dollar as they can.

Interestingly, "price deals can influence the speed of consumption even when the food has already been purchased. This should not, in theory, influence consumption because the cost cannot be recovered, no matter when, or how quickly, the food is consumed. Nevertheless, studies have found that people accelerate the consumption of products perceived to have been purchased at a lower price."

Observation: Quantity discounts lead to stockpiling which accelerates consumption. The quantity purchase of some foods displaces the purchase of other foods. Because it occupies shelf space, we eat more of it. This effect persists even six months after the initial discount.

Recommendation: Offer a buy one, get one free deal. (However, the discounts on healthy food did not reduce purchases of unhealthy food. So, if you want people to buy healthy foods, do not discount unhealthy foods.)

Observation: Consumers prefer price discounts to bonus pack on "vice" foods, but prefer bonus packs to price discounts on healthy food.

Recommendation: Offer free-quantity promotions. That means larger package size on healthy foods such as fruit and vegetables.

The points that are important to food retailers in order to increase sales and profits are the following:

1. Keep the packaging of "vice" foods to smallest sizes and lower the price.
2. Package healthy foods in larger quantities and keep the prices higher.

Building a brand in order to command higher prices takes time and money and is a long-term strategy. For most small companies, branding is an expensive journey to achieve higher prices. It is also a wrong-headed approach to engineering a profit.

You can charge for super quality every day. Branding takes time. Offering super quality and super service builds a loyal customer base faster than raining money on branding and marketing.

The brand follows what you offer. Persistence is the key; persistence in providing top-quality service and products. The reward for having a good brand is a customer list high of quality buyers who love you and this translates into higher valuations when the time comes to sell your enterprise.

Chapter 7
Pricing Strategies Based on Customer Behavior(s)

In this chapter I explain some types of pricing strategies that rely on customer perceptions and behaviors. These are reference pricing, proportional price valuations, perceived fairness, price dripping, gain-loss framing, and finally how, in general, men and women buy differently.

1. Reference Pricing

Reference pricing explains how adding a premium product to a line of products may not mean more sales of the premium product but will stimulate customers to, ultimately, buy the medium-priced product.

Consumers are often bad at math but are wired to compare. There are three broad reasons why reference pricing works. First, consumers know only a few prices so broadly speaking they don't know what anything should cost, so all of us rely on parts of our brains that aren't strictly quantitative. Secondly, although humans spend in numbers (dollars), we make decisions based on clues and half-thinking that amount to a numerical value. Thirdly, we like simple choices and avoiding complications.

When we use reference pricing we are encouraging the use of that shortcut faculty by placing easy-to-compare items in the same group to make a decision happen. Of course, for most companies, this means a comparison on dollars per hour or unit. Successful companies with a deliberate pricing strategy highlight value before price, forcing the customer to put weight on issues of convenience, stress relief, or social status first.

Let's say you walk into a Starbucks and see two deals for a cup of coffee. The first deal offers 33 percent extra coffee free. The second takes 33 percent off the regular price. What's the better deal?

"They're about equal!" you'd say and you would be wrong! The deals appear to be equivalent, but in fact, a 33 percent discount is the same as a 50 percent increase in quantity. Math time: Let's say the standard coffee is $1 for 3 quarts ($0.33 per quart). The first deal gets you 4 quarts for $1 ($0.25 per quart) and the second gets you 3 quarts for 66 cents ($.22 per quart).

How does this explain reference pricing? Getting something extra "for free" often feels better than getting the same for less. The applications of this simple fact are huge. Selling cereal? Don't talk up the discount. Talk about how much bigger the box is! Selling a car? Skip the MPG conversion. Talk about all the extra miles.

In a US experiment, people were offered two kinds of beer: premium beer for $2.50 and bargain beer for $1.80. Around 80 percent chose the more expensive beer. Then, a third beer was introduced, a super bargain beer for $1.60 in addition to the previous two. Now 80 percent bought the $1.80 beer and the rest $2.50 beer. Nobody bought the cheapest option.

On the third time around, they removed the $1.60 beer and replaced with a super premium $3.40 beer. Most people chose the $2.50 beer, a small number $1.80 beer and around 10 percent opted for the most expensive $3.40 beer.

When Williams-Sonoma added a $429 breadmaker next to their $279 model, sales of the cheaper model doubled even though practically nobody bought the $429 machine. The lesson is that if you can't sell a product, try putting something nearly identical, but twice as expensive, next to it. It'll make the first product look like a must-have bargain. One explanation for why this tactic works is that people like stories or justifications. Since it's terribly hard to know the true value of things, we need narratives to explain our decisions to ourselves and our significant others. Price differences give us a story and a motive.

2. Proportional Price Evaluations

Proportional price evaluations examine how customers perceive "price plus free stuff," versus a discounted price, although they are financially identical.

Buyers tend to evaluate price differences proportionally rather than in absolute terms. For example, one research study asked customers if they would leave a store and go to one nearby to save $5 on a purchase. Of respondents who were told that the price in the first store was $15, some 68 percent said they would go to the other store to buy the product for $10. Of respondents who were told that the price in the first store was $125, only 29 percent would switch stores to buy the product for $120. Similar studies have replicated this effect, including research with business manager respondents. When the $5 difference was proportionally 33 percent of the lower price it was more motivating to save the money than when it was proportionally a small part, or 4 percent of the higher price.

Psychologists call the tendency to evaluate price differences proportionately the Weber-Fechner law. It has clear implications for price communication.

For example, auto companies increased the motivational power of their rebate promotions when they offered the option of free financing instead of a fixed-dollar rebate only. Despite the fact that the present value of the interest saved was no more, and often less, than the value of the fixed-dollar rebate, free financing proved more popular. Why? Because eliminating 100 percent of the financing cost motivated consumers more than a 5 percent discount on a $20,000 car. Similarly, hotel chains have found it more effective to offer free breakfast or free Internet access with their rooms than offer a slightly lower price.

This has repercussions on sales and discounting. An important implication of Weber-Fechner is that price change perceptions depend on the percentage, not the absolute difference, and that there are thresholds above and below a product's price at which price changes are noticed or ignored. A series of smaller price increases below the upper threshold is more successful than one large increase. Conversely, buyers respond more to one large price cut below the lower threshold than to a series of smaller, successive discounts. For example, one full-service brokerage house raised its commissions every six months over a three-year period with little resistance from customers. Seeing this success, its competitor tried to match these increases in one large step and received intense criticism.

Studies of consumer markets show that discounts of less than 10 percent elicit hardly any customer response. Offers between 10 and 12 percent exhibited a correlation between discount and sales in more than half the cases recorded. Discounts in excess of 13 percent were distinctly linked to increased sales. The larger the discount, the less likely it was that the brand would maintain its increased share of the market afterwards. The exception is NO TAX sales, even when the offered discount is less than 10 percent. People don't like paying taxes.

3. Perceived Fairness

The concept of a fair price has bedeviled marketers for centuries. In the Middle Ages, merchants were put to death for exceeding public norms regarding the just price. Even in modern market economies, putative price gougers often face press criticism, regulatory hassles, and public boycotts. Consequently, marketers should understand and attempt to manage perceptions of fairness.

What is fair? The concept of fairness appears to be totally unrelated to issues of supply and demand. Assumptions about the seller's profitability influence perceived fairness, but not entirely. Oil companies have often been accused of gouging, even when their profits are below average. When Hurricane Katrina disrupted gasoline supplies in the American south, gas station owners who raised prices were criticized as price gougers even though they had only enough supply to serve those who wanted the product at that price. In contrast to the situation faced by oil companies, popular forms of entertainment (Disney World, for example, or state lotteries) are very profitable and expensive, yet their pricing escapes widespread criticism.

Recent research (*The Strategy and Tactics of Pricing*) seems to indicate that perceptions of fairness are more subjective, and therefore more manageable, than one might otherwise think. Buyers apparently start by comparing what they think is the seller's likely margin and what the seller earned in the past, or to what others earn in similar purchase contexts. In an experiment, people imagined that they were lying on the beach, thirsty for a favorite brand of beer, and that a friend was walking to a nearby location and would bring back beer if the price was not too high. Researchers asked them to specify the maximum amount that they would pay. The subjects did not know that half of them had been told that the friend would patronize a fancy resort hotel while the other half had been told that the friend would buy from a small grocery store. Although these individuals would not themselves visit or enjoy the amenities of the purchase location, the median acceptable price of those who expected the beer to come from the hotel — $2.65 — was dramatically higher than the median acceptable price given by those who expected it to come from the grocery store ($1.50).

Presumptions about the seller's motive influence customers' perceived fairness judgments. A seller justifying a higher price with a "good" motive (e.g., funding, employee health insurance, improving service levels) makes the price more acceptable than does a "bad" motive (e.g., exploiting a market shortage to increase stockholder profits). Just think about the Girl Guide/Girl Scout cookies bought at hugely inflated prices in support of their activities. Research suggests that companies such as Disney with good reputations are much more likely to get the benefit of the doubt about their motives. Those with unpopular reputations (e.g., oil companies) are likely to find their motives suspect.

Finally, perceptions of fairness seem to be related to whether the price is paid to maintain a standard of living, or is paid to improve a standard of living. People consider products that maintain a standard to be necessities, although humanity as probably survived without them for most of its history. Charging a high price for a necessity is generally considered unfair. For example, people object to high prices for life-saving drugs because they feel that they shouldn't have to pay to be healthy. After all, they were healthy last year without having to buy prescriptions and medical advice. People react similarly to rent increases. Yet, the same individuals might buy a new car, jewelry, or a vacation without objecting to equally high prices or price increases.

Fortunately, perceptions of fairness can be managed. Companies that frequently adjust prices to reflect supply and demand or to segment buyers with different price sensitivities are careful to set the regular price at the highest possible level, rather than at the average or most common price. This enables them to discount when necessary to move product at slow times (a "good" motive), rather have to increase prices when demand is strong (a "bad" motive). This works with setting a high Manufacturer's Suggested Retail Price (MSRP) and discounting from that. Similarly, because buyers believe that companies should not have to lose money, it's often best to blame price increases on rising costs to serve customers. Buyers believe that is fair, such as when petroleum prices increase. Landlords who raise rents should announce property improvements at the same time. Innovative companies raise prices more successfully when they are launching a new product and say they are recovering development costs.

4. Price Dripping

Price dripping happens where the price is only partially revealed at first and extras are added as the customer explores. This is often the case with software where the modules and functionality are added for extra charges.

Price dripping relies on getting an initial commitment from which it is difficult to extract yourself, having made a commitment in money and then time to learn the software.

5. Gain-Loss Framing

A final consideration in price communication is presenting the price to customers, who tend to evaluate prices in terms of gains or losses from an expected price point. How they frame those judgments affects the attractiveness of the purchase. To illustrate this effect, grounded in prospect theory, ask yourself which of the following two gas stations you'd be more willing to patronize, assuming that you deem both brands to be equally good and you would always pay with a credit card:

- Station A sells gasoline for $2.20 per gallon, but gives a $0.20 per gallon discount if the buyer pays with cash.

- Station B sells gasoline for $2.00 per gallon, but charges a $0.20 per gallon surcharge if the buyer pays with a credit card.

Of course, the economic cost of buying gasoline from either station is identical. Yet, most people find the offer from station A more attractive than the offer from Station B. The reason is that people place more psychological importance on avoiding losses than on capturing equal size gains. Also, both the gains and losses of an individual transaction are subject, independently, to diminishing returns, as one would expect from the Weber-Fechner law we discussed earlier. A given change has less psychological impact the larger the base to which it is added or subtracted.

In our gas station example, cash buyers prefer A where they receive the psychological benefit of earning a discount, a gain to them. Paying the same $2.00 net price per gallon at station B, which offers no explicit discount, does not provide a psychological benefit.

Credit card buyers also prefer station A, mainly because station B's credit card surcharge creates a loss, a negative psychological benefit to be avoided. Paying the same $2.20 net price per gallon at station A, which requires no explicit surcharge, does not provide a psychological benefit, positive or negative.

Buyers otherwise indifferent to paying by cash or credit will not be indifferent to stations A or B despite the sellers' economic value equivalence; such buyers would always pay cash to get the lowest price but would likely choose A to the psychological satisfaction unavailable at B.

6. Gender Differences in Pricing

If you were lucky enough to listen to the January 14, 2012, Terry O'Reilly broadcast, *Under The Influence* on CBC Radio, you would have been treated to a discourse on aspects of marketing related to knowing your customer.

O'Reilly reports that there is a clear difference in buying patterns between men and women, buying singly and in pairs. Women are more price conscious than men. A woman by herself will shop for bargains and price points. But two women together will pay even less for goods. Moreover, women in pairs appear to treat shopping as an enjoyable Olympic event. The biggest complaint that women have is that they get no help while shopping.

Men, on the other hand, are not as price sensitive and will zero in strategically on the item they want, buy it, and leave. Men do not like to shop in pairs but when they do there is competition to show who is the dominant and more powerful . This urge can take the form of buying a better and more expensive product. Men shopping in pairs pay higher prices than men singly. The biggest complaint of men shopping is that parking is not close enough to the entrance.

7. Prospect Theory

Prospect theory is a theory in cognitive psychology that describes the way people choose between probabilistic alternatives that involve risk, where the probabilities of outcomes are uncertain. The theory states that people make decisions based on the potential value of losses and gains rather than the final outcome, and that people evaluate these losses and gains using some mental shortcuts. The model is descriptive: it tries to model real-life choices, rather than optimal decisions, as normative models do.

Prospect theory has many implications for price communication:

- To make prices less objectionable, make them opportunity costs (gains forgone) rather than out-of-pocket costs. Banks often waive fees for checking accounts in return for maintaining a minimum balance. Even when the interest forgone on the funds in the account exceeds the charge for checking, most people choose the minimum balance option. People find it less painful to pay for things such as insurance or mutual funds with payroll deductions instead of buying them outright.

- When your product is priced differently to different customers and at different times, set the list price at the highest level and give most people discounts. This type of pricing is so common that we take it for granted. Colleges, for example charge only a small portion of customers the list price and give everyone else discounts. To those who pay at or near the full price, the failure to receive more of a discount (a gain forgone) is much less objectionable than if they were asked to pay a premium because they are not star students, athletes, or good negotiators

- Unbundle gains and bundle losses. Many companies sell offerings consisting of many individual products and services. For example, a printing company not only prints brochures but also helps design the job, matches colors, schedules the job to meet the buyer's time requirements, and so on. To maximize the perceived value, the seller could identify each of these as a separate product or service and promote the value of each one explicitly ("Look at all you get in our Deluxe Package!"), unbundling the gains. However, rather than asking the buyer to make individual expenditure decisions, the seller could identify the customer's needs and offer a package price to meet them ("One price brings all to you"), bundling the loss. If the buyer objects to the price, the seller can take away a service, which will then make that service appear as standalone "loss" that will be hard to give up. (*The Strategy and Tactics of Pricing: A Guide to Growing More Profitably*, Routledge, 2005.)

- Offer memberships instead of one-time fees. We're pained by transaction costs and we are drawn to subscriptions and memberships and bundles partially because we seek to avoid transaction costs. We'd rather overpay a little than suffer the psychological pain of pulling out a wallet and watching our money go to each gym season, hockey season, or movie.

8. Using Customer Behaviors to Benefit Your Profits

Customer behavior is not always rational. For decades, economists have struggled to make Homo Economicus, an ideal of a rational objective decision maker, fit the real world. But it failed in the face of the reality of customers paying high prices, buying what they don't need, philanthropy, and altruism.

Understanding why customers respond to how prices, products, and services are presented opens up huge profit opportunities.

The lessons are not always clear and will warp in different industries.

Reference pricing works because it relies on the reptilian side of our brains and not the calculating part when comparing discounts and benefits.

Proportional pricing works because a price can be framed to position small disadvantages in a positive light.

Price framing is often industry-specific and understanding that, you can be seen favorably in a crowd of blackguards.

Price dripping works for certain industries; online software providers and service providers for example.

Gain-loss framing works because we can portray all company claims in terms of benefits and penalties.

Prospect theory helps us understand that risk is an essential part of a buying decision and minimizing it helps us get our dream price.

Finally, men and women buy differently so your transaction opportunities should reflect the behavioral differences.

Chapter 8
The Failure of Conventional Pricing

Conventional methods of pricing are simple but lead to mediocre results. For small businesses these are often the only pricing strategies they know. They leave money on the table and here is why.

1. WAG, SWAG, and STICK Methods

In so many small businesses, the price of goods and services is often based on guesswork: the Wild Ass Guess (WAG) method, Scientific Wild Ass Guess (SWAG), where there are some numbers to back up the guesswork, or STICK where every stick and nail is costed.

WAG is often used by those who have long experience in the industry or trade. This is an experience-based method for pricing where trial and costly errors have already taken place. If, for the past ten years, it has cost $5,000 to renovate a bathroom, then presumably it will always cost $5,000 to renovate a bathroom. Faced with creeping labor costs or perhaps sudden spikes in the price of plumbing fixtures, this method is frequently unable to change. Faced with a new competitor in the market that is willing to undertake the same bathroom renovation for $3,500, the WAG method practitioner does not know how to respond properly. There is simply too much information that must be kept in the estimator's head to stay current and remain competitive yet profitable. Worse yet, estimators are human and tend to respond to the last comment they had from a customer. If that comment was negative because the customer thought the price was too high, then the price on the next job will drop. If the business owner is also the estimator, then the price can reflect not value to the customer or even costs, but the state of the bank account at the time.

There is a deeper concern that the WAG skill is not easy to transfer because it cannot be written down. In most small businesses where the owner of the company is the estimator, this skill and knowledge is largely not transferable to employees or a new owner. That implies that the business will be undervalued when so much of the company's way of doing business is buried in the owner's head. When the time comes for the owner to retire, therefore, the price will reflect that hurdle and the potential for the value of the sale will likely be lower.

The SWAG method, as the name implies, has some numbers to back up the experience based approach. "OK, so that job will take four men five days to complete and I pay them $20 per hour. With labor cost at $3,200 and adding a third for materials and then a third for profit, that should be about it." This rough and ready method does not take into account travel time, overhead and management costs, payroll taxes, nor fudge factor in case things go wrong. This job might actually lose money.

The STICK method is the name given to the clumsy and time consuming method of working out the costs of each and every nail, foot of strapping, two-by-four, can of paint, and labor to the nearest 15 minutes to arrive at a total cost. It is very time consuming and does not produce better sales response from the customer. In fact, the delay in getting quotes back to customers can be the sole deciding issue on whether or not your company gets the job.

STICK is, in fact, an adaptation of industrial manufacturing cost accounting methods to service providers and custom builders. It can take place on paper and I have also seen some very elaborate spreadsheets meant to cope with the vast amount of information. The advantage to this method is that, having gone to the trouble of detailing every aspect of this "virtual build" is that, if and when the customer says OK, you have a bill of materials for the purchaser and a plan for the carpenters.

There are two principal disadvantages to the STICK method. First is the speed factor. If you are an estimator for a home renovation company for example, you must make a minimum of two visits to the site plus perhaps several phone calls before you have an answer. There is always the feeling among business owners and estimators I have talked with that some estimates are just a waste of time but they must go through this drawn-out procedure just because they were asked for a quote.

Second is that, having committed so much time and effort to the quote, the price is not easily altered to reflect customer expectations. In other words, if the quote is $7,000 and the customer's budget does not extend beyond $5,000, you cannot easily and quickly find the savings to meet the value expectation. There is simply too much information on the table to alter the quote simply and easily. The only line item that can easily be altered is the profit line and doing so may mean the job makes no money. What a dilemma!

2. Cost-Based Pricing

We are taught very early in our lives and again in our business careers that price is a derivative of costs. After all, an item selling for $25 must have a cost near to some fraction of that price. Moreover, that fraction should bear some resemblance to a mathematically provable cost and markup structure that generates reasonable profit for the company. Cost + profit = price.

Fortunately, the reality is a bit different. Fortunately because the difference leads to better profit opportunities.

In history, fortunes were made by pricing an item without regard to cost. For example, nails used to be made by hand. Nails were a coveted item. When the Chamberlain family of Birmingham developed and deployed nail making machines, the machines spewed out hundreds of thousands of machine-made nails in minutes. The Chamberlains set the price at a percentage of the handmade price and not as a derivative of cost. They made a fortune. Eventually, competition drove down the price to where we regard nails as nearly worthless.

Wang Labs, founded in 1951, was a pioneer in word processors and calculators. At its height it had 33,000 employees and $3 billion in sales. When the market became really competitive in the '80s the accountants instructed management to increase prices because profits were down. Price increases drove down volumes and profits took another hit. Again, the accountants advised a price increase. Eventually, the company failed.

To go to a modern example, consider the price of tiny capacitors used in all manner of electronic devices. They can be priced as low as a quarter of a cent. An iPhone has 100 of these inside it. The price of a

Why Do Prices End in 99 cents?

The phenomenon of 99 cent pricing seems to have first become common in the nineteenth century, shortly after the invention of the cash register. The cash register was a remarkable innovation; not only did it do simple arithmetic, it also kept a record of every sale. That's important if you think your employees might be stealing from you. You can examine the tape at the end of the day and know how much money should be in the drawer.

There is one small problem with cash registers. They don't actually record every sale; they record only those sales that area rung up. If a customer buys an item for $1 and hands the clerk a dollar bill, the clerk can neglect to record the sale, slip the dollar in his or her pocket, and leave no one the wiser.

capacitor is irrelevant compared to the loss of use of an iPhone due to failure of this small component. So the manufacturers choose a supplier not on price but on reliability.

From my own experience, I was installing a small local area network (LAN) in my business. In those days, computers were linked together with coaxial cable. I had spent $10,000 in 1980s dollars, when I was asked to purchase the final component: a metal box the size of a cigarette package that connected all the wires together and made the system work. It was, if I recall correctly, $300. I paid. My system worked. When, a few months later, the magic box failed, I opened it up to find two crossed transistors inside that I recognized from my own inventory. My cost to replace the transistors was 25 cents.

In setting a pricing strategy, costs come into play only when considering the minimum viable price point and determining a return on investment on all assets deployed. Don't let your accountant set the prices.

3. Margin Pricing

Most companies and accountants use margin calculations (the difference between cost and sales) as a yardstick to measure a company's performance since it links together the sales and price with raw costs; the primary way the company makes its money. It is a simple and comfortable way to measure.

Unfortunately, its simplicity creates a host of potential problems for the simple reason that price is determined by many more factors than a math problem.

The first problem is that it emphasizes costs and not value. We have already seen leaving value off the table ignores the entire opportunity of market segmentation and the extra profits generated by that extra work. Business owners are leaving money on the table by not understanding the value to the customer of what they are offering.

Moreover, a fixed margin target ignores that a customer's needs change and that your product or service may be offering greater and greater value to your customers.

Second, margin focus assumes that your clients are all clones. Do you treat all of your customers the same, making the assumptions that they all have identical needs and identical wallets? If so, you miss opportunity for greater profits. Consider that the buyer of ink cartridges could be students, business owners, purchasing agents, and government offices. The needs are not the same. Consider that an emergency hot water tank replacement on a Sunday evening has more value than an appointment scheduled two weeks in advance.

Third, a focus on margins assumes that all your products and services are all clones. Are your difficult to find inventory items priced to the same margin calculation as goods easily available at any hardware store?

Finally, a focus only on margins means that you can only increase revenues and profits by increasing sales. That is really easy, isn't it? But, a pricing strategy can increase profits overnight.

4. Risk and Return

A familiar story in the construction trades is to attach a tariff to flow-through charges to cover the costs of paperwork and gain a little profit. Your customer needs a plumber and you bring one in, attach 10 percent to the bill and get an easy few dollars on the transaction. It seems like a good idea. Many times it works. However, all of the time there is a risk (who is responsible to your customer?) if the job goes sideways. There is a risk attached to these transactions and it needs to be weighed carefully and wisely.

Suppose that you had the chance to cut a check for $1,000 that represented your entire out-of-pocket expenses. For the $1,000 you could buy an option to purchase a house for $270,000, but the house is really worth $340,000. Would you do it?

The ratio of risk to reward is low. The risk is the nonrefundable deposit taken: $1,000 from your bank account. The house will never evaporate and in most cases not depreciate. Moreover, you are buying the house at below list value. The reward factor is measurable.

Let us suppose that you had a chance to cut a similar check for a $1,000 in return for the chance to buy stocks in a company about which you knew nothing except that the promoter tells you it will hit the heavens?

The risk to reward ratio is high and without further homework, you should probably feel queasy about signing that check.

How does this apply to pricing? Having a shrewd perception of the downside of a contract may help you make good business decisions rather than fatal ones. An appreciation of the risk may persuade you not to change the overall value of the package of goods and services but rather to unbundle them to reflect your risk and rewards.

In other words, how can you legitimately give value to your customer in providing services or products outside your normal course of business and see some of the profit for doing so hit your bank account? At the same time, how can you place a wall between you and the outside provider so that his or her poor performance or bad luck does not have a disastrous impact on your business?

During the hot property market years in British Columbia, a kitchen design company employed the standard business model of selling an entire kitchen design, buying the cabinets, installing the cabinets, and putting a markup of a few points on the cabinets and the installation. The cabinet manufacturer demanded 100 percent of the cabinet price on delivery but was frequently late especially for small customers like my client.

On first examination, it appeared that the designer would have a $6,000 job profit on a $35,000 job; a 17 percent profit margin. On a job sheet or a profit and loss statement, it would be difficult to find fault with this model. However, when you considered the cash flow and the market circumstances the picture changed horribly.

First, the dollars paid to the manufacturer for the cabinets — $20,000 — came from the customer's initial deposit. The entire customer deposit had been used to buy the cabinets.

In order to complete the job, the company had to use its own cash reserves to cover the cost of installation and design. This was a cash flow nightmare for my client. When the cabinet manufacturers did not deliver on time (a frequent occurrence); or delivered only a portion of the cabinets ordered — almost 90 percent of the time — the customers were understandably unhappy. If the customers demanded their money back — and they did — the company did not have the cash reserves to comply.

Even if the company fought to get around this difficulty; upon completion a significant number of customers refused to pay the 10 percent holdback on the entire job: $3,500 or 58 percent of the entire anticipated profit.

The risk-return ratio was wrong for the market circumstances; the unreliability of the cabinet makers.

In remedying this problem, the business model had to be turned on its head by unbundling the transaction and getting the profit paid first. (See Figure 10.)

Initially, the customer paid the company for a kitchen design. This translated into $8,000 in revenue that paid for the design, overheads,

Company cost of the cabinets	$20,000	
Installation at cost	$4,000	
Design at cost	$5,000	
Total cost kitchen renovation	$29,000	
Markup on the cabinets	$2,000	10%
Markup on installation	$1,000	25%
Markup on design	$3,000	60%
Total expected profit	$6,000	
Total price kitchen renovation	$35,000	
Customer deposit	$20,000	57%
Anticipated profit on this job	$6,000	17%
10% holdback by the customer	$3,500	58% of total profit

Figure 10: Before: The Revenue Model

and the owners. All of the profit to be expected from this transaction was paid up front plus $2,000 for future costs.

Then the customers were introduced to the manufacturer from whom they bought the cabinets directly. Blame for late or incomplete deliveries therefore came home to roost with the manufacturer and the designer could commiserate but never took the blame.

When the time came for the installation, it was paid by the customer to the company and the company paid the installer.

Even better, the design company got a sales commission from the manufacturer, which dropped promptly to the bottom line.

Company cost of the cabinets	$0	
Installation at cost	$4,000	
Design at cost	$5,000	
Total cost kitchen renovation	$9,000	
Markup on the cabinets	$2,000	
Markup on installation	$1,000	25%
Markup on design	$3,000	60%
Total expected profit	$6,000	
Total price kitchen renovation	$15,000	
Customer deposit	$13,500	
Anticipated profit on this job	$6,000	67%
10% holdback by the customer	$1,500	25% of total profit

Figure 11: After: The Revenue Model

From a price point of view, the cost to the customer did not change. However, a perception of extra value did emerge. In the first place, the customers believed the designer was getting them the manufacturer's best price and since they paid the manufacturer directly, they were not being "taxed" by the designer. The customer paid for performance and the designer put together a beautiful kitchen and was paid. When the cabinets arrived, the installer was paid. Even with a normal holdback the risk to actual profit was minor.

The result? Without the flow-through cabinet revenue, sales dropped by two thirds, but profits rose by four times.

So, in your business, are you risking large amounts of cash on deals that stand a chance of going sideways? What is the realistic risk? Will it cripple your company? How do you avoid it?

Old version	
Total cost	$35,000
New version	
Cost of design and installation	$15,000
Cost of cabinets	$20,000
Total costs	$35,000

Figure 12: Customer Pricing

5. Don't Be Afraid to Charge What You Are Worth and Change How You Do Things

An academic study of the Wisconsin wine industry (Yes, Tommy, there is a Wisconsin wine industry) began its analysis by stating that the biggest problem facing the industry was the fear of charging higher prices. Be brave and charge what your products or services are really worth. Customers will leave if you are not offering value, give poor customer service, or your product is low quality.

Look at your current pricing strategy and dissect its rationale. Very often the strategy is, from my consulting experience, built on assumptions that are outdated and leave money on the table. Since pricing is the last frontier for profit engineering, it is worth every minute spent to modernize your methods.

Worksheet 6
Position Your Price

At what price would our customer not consider buying your offering?

At what price would your product or service be expensive but your customers still buy it?

At what price would your product be inexpensive?

At what price does the pricing become so inexpensive that your customer questions its value?

What price would be the most acceptable?

How will you segment the market and offer different prices to different customers?

How much volume can you afford to lose due to a price increase and still maintain profit levels?

Chapter 9
Successful Pricing Strategies

1. Price Optimization

Price optimization is the use of mathematical analysis by a person, company, or software to determine how customers will respond to different prices for its products and services through different channels. We should be applying this kind of scientific rigor to the process of setting prices; in doing so prices will be tweaked often. The methods of exchange today are largely the same as they were in medieval times — most sellers guess what buyers will buy, guess who will buy it, guess at what price they can sell it, and apply a sticker. This guessing hurts both seller and buyer. I believe that the seller should try to match the price to the buyer's willingness to pay and perception of value. Knowing and expressing the value proposition is the key here and then lending a keen ear to the customer's needs. That approach is more time consuming than conventional methods but will yield more profitable results.

How do you set your prices? With ad hoc, last-minute pricing meetings or with a more stringent process? What data does the company use? Cost and gut feel are the most common answers.

The results are prices that are hit or miss; mostly miss. Mostly we see prices that leave money on the table as well as reduce sales. At best, these ad hoc meetings may come up with a price that kind of works, but they do not allow companies to develop optimal prices.

So what then is optimal pricing? Well, every prospective customer of a company has a certain willingness to pay. This willingness to pay is influenced by many things: the tangible and intangible benefits of the product or service the prospect is about to buy; the competitive landscape; other alternative precuts or services; the urgency the prospect has to solve the problem the product or service solves; and, of course, access to funds.

Optimal prices allow a company to capture the maximum available from every prospective customer's willingness to pay.

Optimal prices help your customers select the specific products and levels of service they are willing to pay for.

Optimizing prices really makes a huge difference to the business's results. In fact, companies that optimized their prices have, on average, twice the profitability, twice the growth rate, and four to five times the valuation when compared to companies that don't. Optimizing prices is surprisingly easy to do, but you do need the data.

2. Seven Questions for Price Optimization

Which of the statements below best applies to you? If most of these items are checked, then your prices are optimal, and you likely capture the maximum possible percentage of your prospect's willingness to pay. Most likely you are the leader in your industry. If not, and if you aspire to become the leader in your industry, or at least improve your sales level and profit margin, Checklist 1 will help you view your pricing differently, and inspire you to take action to begin harnessing the power of price optimization.

3. Optimizing Pricing for Limited-Time and/or Limited-Inventory Offers

Online retailers can offer limited-time discounts ("flash sales") to create a feeling of urgency and scarcity of products by offering great deals, but only for a limited time (often a few days) and with limited inventory. Frequently, websites show the customer a number of "events" each representing a collection of similar products. Each event shows a countdown timer offering the customer of the time remaining in the sale. ("The New Frontier of Price Optimization," *Frontiers Research*, September, 2017.)

Checklist 1
Optimized Pricing

- ☐ Have you any evidence about how much your customers are willing to pay for your products or services?

- ☐ Do you have any data to show how price levels influence sales volumes for your most important products or services?

- ☐ Do you know which market segments are most successful with your products and services, and which are the most profitable to sell to and to serve?

- ☐ Have you analyzed your historical sales transaction data to find correlations and dependencies between products and between services, and do you take pricing action based on these findings?

- ☐ Do you use a different pricing and discount strategy for products and services that are unique, than you use for products or services that are competitive, or even commodities?

- ☐ Do you know how you can use your price structure to increase willingness to buy and willingness to pay over time?

- ☐ Are your salespeople good at selling value?

These are the main points to check in order to optimize prices. If your pricing today is driven mostly by gut feelings or guesswork, optimized pricing will have a profound impact on your company.

The flash sale concept was also used in a pub near Vancouver, BC. Struggling to find its market, the owner, Ted, was straying from the original concept of being a haven for beer snobs. I pulled in a concept from a free house I frequented in London. Free houses are not tied to a particular brewery and can buy from anywhere. The Sun pub frequently had "guest" beers, limited issue kegs bought from the overflow stock of local breweries. You never knew from visit to visit what may be on tap.

So Ted ran with the idea, calling all the local breweries and buying surplus inventory. With the help of social media, the crowds of beer snobs arrived to sample new and interesting beer.

4. Activity-Based Costing (ABC) and Activity-Based Pricing (ABP)

Traditionally, cost accountants arbitrarily added a broad percentage onto the direct costs (materials and labor, etc.), to allow for the indirect (freight, taxes, etc.) costs.

Worksheet 7
Seven Questions for Price Optimization

Which of the statements below best applies to you? If you can answer most of these items with a "yes," then your prices are optimal, and you likely capture the maximum possible percentage of your prospects' willingness to pay. Most likely you are the leader in your industry. If not, and if you aspire to become the leader in your industry, or at least improve your sales level and profit margin, this list will help you view your pricing differently, and inspire you to take action to begin harnessing the power of price optimization.

1. Have you any proof, beyond a gut feel, as to how much your customers are willing to pay for your products or services?

2. Do you have any data on how price levels influence sales volumes for your most important products or services?

3. Have you collected any data on which market segments are most successful with your products and services, and which are the most profitable to sell to and to serve?

4. Have you analyzed your historical sales transaction data to find correlations and dependencies between products and between services, and do you take pricing action based on these findings?

5. Do you use a different pricing and discount strategy for products and services that are unique, than you use for products or services that are competitive, or even commodities?

6. Do you know how you can use your price structure to increase willingness to buy and willingness to pay over time?

7. Are your salespeople good at selling value?

However, as the percentages of overhead costs rose, this technique became increasingly inaccurate because the indirect costs were not caused equally by all the products. For example, one product might take more time in an expensive machine than another product, but since the amount of direct labor and materials might be the same, the additional cost for the use of the machine would not be recognized when the same broad percentage is added to all products. Consequently, when multiple products share common costs, there is a danger of one product subsidizing another.

The concepts of Activity-Based Costing (ABC) were developed in the manufacturing sector of the United States during the 1970s and 1980s. During this time, the Consortium for Advanced Manufacturing-International, now known simply as CAM-I, provided a formative role for studying and formalizing the principles that have become this method, more formally known as ABC.

Instead of using broad arbitrary percentages to allocate costs, ABC seeks to identify cause-and-effect relationships to assign costs objectively. Once costs of the activities have been identified, the cost of each activity can be attributed to each product to the extent that the product uses the activity. In this way ABC often identifies areas of high overhead costs per unit and so directs attention to finding ways to reduce the costs or to charge more for costly products.

Like manufacturing industries, financial institutions also have diverse products which can cause cross-product subsidies. Since personnel expenses represent the largest single component of noninterest expense in financial institutions, these costs must also be attributed more accurately to products and customers. Activity-based costing, even though developed for manufacturing, can be a useful tool for doing this.

Direct labor and materials are relatively easy to trace directly to products, but it is more difficult to directly allocate indirect costs to products. Where products use common resources differently, some sort of weighting is needed in the cost allocation process. The measure of the use of a shared activity by each of the products is known as the cost driver. For example, the cost of the activity of bank tellers can be ascribed to each product by measuring how long each product's transactions takes at the counter and then by measuring the number of each type of transaction.

Three things can happen when establishing a product price. A price set too high is a lost sale that could have been profitable at a lower price. A price set too low is rewarded with unprofitable work. Only when a price is set appropriately does a company make both a sale and a profit. Just as activity-based costing and activity-based management revolutionized the cost accounting world, activity-based pricing (ABP) brings a disciplined approach to developing pricing. Activity-based pricing examines the relationships between price, cost, and sales volume and how this relationship affects profitability.

So the question to ask is whether all of your customers are profitable. After you add the costs to serve low margin customers, are they still profitable? Do your high margin customers demand so much from you that they are not profitable?

Are all customers equally profitable? Of course not. Some customers behave like saints and others like sinners.

4.1 Questions you need to answer about your products and customers

Certain questions should be asked about your products and customers in order to do proper costing and pricing:

- Do we push for volume or margin with a specific customer?
- Are there ways to improve profitability by altering the package of products or services we sell to that customer?
- Does the sales volume justify the discounts we give that customer?
- Can we change that customer to our new profit directed strategy?

4.2 Limitations of ABC

Even in activity-based costing, some overhead costs are difficult to assign to products and customers; for example, the chief executive's salary.

These costs are termed "business sustaining" and are not assigned to products and customers because there is no meaningful method. This lump of unallocated overhead costs must nevertheless be met by contributions from each of the products, but it is not as large as the overhead costs before ABC is employed.

5. Dynamic Pricing (Surge Pricing)

We all know that business absolutely refuses to follow those beautifully consistent budget numbers; that revenues rise and fall day by day and month by month. So, at certain times of the cycle, demand is low and at other times it's high.

We often set prices once and for all, ignoring these demand cycles. What does that mean to profits and sales?

In Figure 13, demand, in bold, rises and falls. The price is a straight line across the time scale. Demand rises above the price line and then dips below the price line.

When demand is high, sales and profits roll in because the price is lower than would be predicted by a simple analysis of demand and supply. When demand dips below the price line, the company is priced out of the market. Below the line is lost sales and above the line is lost profit. Why?

If demand is high and you have the lowest price, you get the business but you have given up a profit opportunity to carry you through the business cycle.

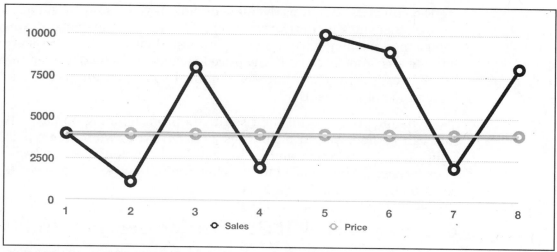

Figure 13: Demand versus Price

If demand is low and your price is high relative to the demand, then no one buys from you and sales go down.

This can be changed. Dynamic pricing takes into account micro changes in demand and adjusts the price accordingly. We have all seen this. Hotels charge a premium in the high summer months but offer bargains in the winter. Want to rent a moving van at month end? Pay the price! Of course, gasoline prices shoot up just before the first long weekend of the summer. Airlines used to reward the late arrivals at the airport by offering best price seating in response to an analysis that it was better to fly with a passenger in the seat at any price than fly empty. Of course, they have since found that this rewarded bad behavior and have reversed the offering, charging more to the last-minute traveler.

On a more sophisticated level, *The Economist* reported the use of dynamic pricing software being used in pubs in London to reflect higher demand during happy hour right after work, versus the slower early evening drinking crowd. Prices moved by the quarter hour.

Dynamic pricing also works for longer time scales.

Every year in western Canada, the lawn mowing season opens in April. Almost immediately, there is a rush to get the mower tuned up or repaired. The wait times can exceed six weeks. One repair shop owner contacted his customer base in the dead of winter and offered immediate service and free storage for machines brought in promptly instead of waiting for the mowing season to begin.

E-commerce often uses dynamic pricing. If you search on Amazon among other sites such as travel websites for a product, their algorithms determine that they have found an interested customer. If you leave this site and come back later, the price may increase a modest amount. Why? Because the algorithm has identified you as an interested customer and not just a surfer.

Dynamic pricing is on the rise. It is a profit building opportunity that can be deployed in businesses as diverse as lawnmower repair, selling beer, hotel rooms and selling gasoline. You don't need software to experiment. You do need to make an attempt and keep detailed records on the results.

6. Data and How It Gets Used to Generate Profits

Grocery stores now have the capacity to text you as you stroll the aisles. Your loyalty card signals that you have arrived and the algorithms roll into action to offer you products. Always buy steak on Thursday? Well, here is a bargain on frozen French fries to go with it.

Do you have a loyalty card? That is the card in your wallet you hand to the cashier because you are promised a loyalty discount from regular retail prices. Grocery stores offer them. Big box stores love them. For years we have understood they are just collecting information on our buying habits.

Our assumption on these buying habits is that businesses can stay in touch with customer changes in buying habits.

For example, when I worked as General Manager in the Cayman Islands for a Costco knockoff, we tracked the purchase of disposal diapers. A shopper buying diapers for a two year old this year would be buying for a three-year-old kid next year. (Funny how they keep growing, right?) It was in our commercial interest to track the numbers sold so that we could have enough inventory for sale next year. This improved our buying habits and kept customers loyal to us.

This is not very insidious. Or is it?

Loyalty cards have two other uses. Your loyalty card is being used to offer regular and heavy users a deeper discount and, therefore, cheaper prices on goods. Nothing to complain about there. The occasional buyer who pops in just once in a while pays a higher price.

Commercially, it makes sense to reward those who patronize your business. The loyalty card allows us to collect the data and manipulate prices to improve profits.

The second use of the loyalty card is by insurance companies which have concluded they can fine tune their insurance products by knowing more about you than is revealed by actuarial tables. You may be a car owner who buys a lot of beer on Fridays and Saturdays. Your habits could be considered to be risky behavior. You could be characterized as being at a greater risk of being involved in a drink-related accident than someone who drives but hardly ever buys booze.

Data mining is still in its infancy. If the information is available, someone will find a use for it. Google proved that.

We have the technical horsepower to track our every activity on a daily basis. We have closed circuit cameras watching our streets and intersections. We have passive credit cards that are read by gas pumps and customs booths. GPS in our smartphones can locate us and track us. Your web camera on your laptop could soon use already developed facial recognition programs. These algorithms interpret your response to certain types of advertisements as you surf the web. If you smile, you get more advertisements.

Dynamic pricing — prices that move up or down in response to changing conditions, changing clientele and the whim of the commercial interest — is here to stay. I will urge you, it is worthwhile experimenting knowledgeably with the techniques.

7. Price Skimming: Lessons in Pricing from Apple

Apple has taught many entrepreneurs the importance of design, how to create buzz when introducing new products to the marketplace, how to pioneer new technology, and the importance of superior quality.

Apple also employs wily pricing experts who have used pricing strategies to create extra profits.

The most recent example is the Apple response to Samsung's huge presence in the Indian market. Apple's products are too pricey for the average Indian, where many people still survive on $2 USD per day. Smartphones make sense in countries where electricity supplies and telecoms infrastructure is weak and prone to frequent blackouts. Phones add value to people's lives by bringing them close to the markets. This has already happened in some poor fishing communities that dot the coastline. When heading back with the catch of the day, they can check the spot prices at various ports within reach and choose the best paying one. Clearly smartphones are an economic accelerator. So, how to get more smartphones into Indian hands?

Apple has used a price skimming strategy for the consumer market. Early adopters pay greatly for the newest and brightest toys. Apple also knows that competitors can enter the market easily and quickly after Apple has pioneered the technology, so constant innovation is a hallmark of Apple products.

That means the earliest smartphones are soon obsolete. Apple could not dump the old phones on the American or early adopter market, for fear of cannibalizing its own consumer segment. So Apple took the older phones to India, effectively buying market share with a great, if outdated product that has already generated all the profits Apple expected.

Not all of us have the luxury of dumping our old products on a foreign market. How can Apple's leadership in this pricing gambit be put to use in a small business?

If your pricing model demands a profit margin on each and every inventory item you sell, you will not be able to sell the end-of-season or dust covered items for a dollar. You will lose money.

Apple has a simple idea. Not all inventory moves equally. If you sell seasonal or fashion products, some product will be left over after the majority has sold. If your pricing model allowed for this hangover — check your records in prior years — then you could sell the leftovers for $1 and make a profit. See my prior articles at www.pricingstrategies.ca on how the big box stores price this way or take a look at my book, *Pricing Strategies for Small Business* (Self-Counsel Press, 2008). If you sell strategically, you can gain new clientele. By contacting your customer list and advising of a tremendous sale, you move inventory that would otherwise gather dust and gain loyal customers at the same time.

8. Pocket Price Banding

Price banding is defined by the upper and lower limit at which goods and services from your company are sold.

"The width and shape of a pocket price band tell a fruitful story. Managers are invariably surprised not only by the width of their pocket price bands but also by the identity of the customers at the extremes of the band." ("Managing price, gaining profit," *Harvard Business Review*, Sept-Oct 1992.)

For example, an Edmonton-based parts wholesaler offered standard payment terms to its customers. Thirty days after the statement was issued, checks came pouring in. Then something funny happened. Sales jumped on the first few days of the month. This was unexpected. Someone buying goods on January 1 had the 31 days of January and the 28 days of February to pay, meaning 60-day terms and not 30. This meant the company had to stretch its cash further every month.

What does this mean? Pocket price is the dollar ending up in the company pocket as true revenue after the price has cascaded from list to customer discount, to early payment discount, to volume rebates, and to free delivery. The very flexibility in the price band means that an identical product will be sold on the same day in the same city at very different prices. The price may vary as much as 25 percent from upper to lower limits as in an extreme case such as the Castle Battery study in the appendix.

Moreover, the Castle Study consultants investigated the supposition that volume pricing to big customers caused the variation and found no such thing. Some legacy clients who bought small amounts were regularly being given pricing similar to that offered to the largest accounts.

How does this happen? It is a familiar story of starting with a price list and then giving some flexibility to the sales force in order to get the sale. When the list price is discounted and then off-invoice costs are added price flexibility becomes the norm rather than the exception. This could be the result of customers knowing your entire sales system too well and working the system to their advantage. Or it could be due to weak selling skills.

9. Bundling and Unbundling

Bundling can solve problems of cash flow, stodgy inventory, and profitability. Typically, this tactic is employed to get slow moving inventory off the shelves by tying the sale to a fast moving item and wrapping everything up in fancy paper as a gift. People will spend more on a gift than on themselves. Christmas gift baskets, to use a simple analogy, are typically created around one or two core and interesting products surrounded by slow movers.

LinkedIn's decision to package some seldom-used features as high-margin "premium" accounts spawned a business line that now makes almost $250 million a year.

You can increase perceived value with better marketing. eBay, for instance, offered a feature from its inception that for 25 cents allowed people who sell products on the site to add a photo next to their listings. It wasn't used much. It turned out that sellers who included the pictures had much higher click rates and tended to command a higher price for their goods. eBay started to market this data along with the feature.

With the benefit of the sales data, eBay's sellers saw that the pictures helped solve a problem and their perceived value skyrocketed.

Because it didn't cost eBay $0.25 to host a photograph, the feature, along with other optional upgrades, eventually generated hundreds of millions a year in pure profits.

This tactic can be employed in services as well. If you are faced with customers to whom only the price per hour you charge is the deciding factor in the buying decision, then creating "price packages" makes it difficult for the customer to compare apples to apples. For example, if your regular charge-out rate is $30 per hour and the potential customer is only mildly interested in the services you have to offer for that price, repackaging at a lump price where the items are carefully delineated with fulsome descriptions could overcome price objections. After all, it is the check that has to be written by the customers that is important here, and with an open-ended, per-hour charge, they do not know the size of the charge until you have finished.

Unbundling is the reverse of the process wherein the series of goods offered are separated and priced separately. Typically this reveals that some service — after-sales service, for example, or a gasket that is always thrown away and never used — can be removed from the package safely and sold separately. This allows for a price decrease to meet stiffer competition or adds to margins in the event that prices are not reduced.

Consider the example of a computer services company as noted in *The Strategy and Tactics of Pricing*. The company was a leader in providing support and software selection but experiencing price erosion due to the entry of a price-driven competitor. Management had perceived this as a pricing problem and prepared to re-create the company as a low-cost provider. Luckily they took a harder look and noted that their pricing structure forced all customers to engage with Techco identically even in the face of wide ranging needs.

Customers who received little value from Techco's services were asked to pay the same price as customers who received full value. The result was that Techco underpriced to its high-value customers and over-priced to its low-value customers.

"The profit maximizing solution to this pricing challenge was not a wholesale reduction in prices. Instead, the solution was to redesign the priced structure in a way that allowed customers to choose how they engaged with Techco. Customers that got little value from Techco's services were not asked to pay for them, nor were they allowed free access to service and support — an important change from past practice. Eliminating support to some customers enabled Techco to increase support to high value customers to justify higher prices. By adopting a comprehensive approach to pricing strategy, Techco was able to increase volume in the low-end segments while improving margins in the high-end segments."

10. What Now?

In this chapter, I have examined several successful pricing strategies.

Any one of these strategies can be deployed in your business. What is important to know about this list is that you can use some of the concepts today to improve your profits.

You will notice that every one of these pricing solutions is more complex to implement than the standard, conventional pricing models. It will take time and effort plus a return loop of data collected to make a business a lot more profitable, but it is worth it.

Chapter 10
Retail Pricing

I have included a chapter exclusively on retail because it is undergoing massive changes due to our ability to collect huge amounts of data on how people buy. This has led to more dynamic or surge pricing strategies than we have seen before. This has also led to the growth of loyalty cards, internet analytics and sophisticated tracking, and highly targeted advertising.

Price is a critical competitive issue for retailers. A recent survey by a Gartner Company subsidiary and a point of sale research firm, Software Advice, examined how retail technology adoption, especially pricing strategy, can help a retailer stay afloat in today's make-or-break market. The report confirmed that retailers face a number of important decisions when determining how to price their goods and services. Setting prices correctly, on the one hand, can attract customers, drive sales, burnish a retailer's reputation, and affect the retailer's very existence. Incorrectly set prices, on the other hand, can have a profoundly negative impact on sales and customer loyalty. To help make more informed decisions, retailers must rely on the use of price monitoring and analysis married to various pricing strategies.

The point of this chapter is to isolate and highlight retail selling which has peculiarities all its own. Retail has more complexity than any other arena. Retail pricing has the most variants and works when there is a deep understanding of the customers who buy.

I went to my local market today and saw a sign that said: ONE WATERMELON FOR $3 OR THREE FOR $10

Instead of telling the guy behind the stall how stupid he was, I decided to show him.

I walked up to him and asked: "Can I buy a watermelon please?"

"Yes sir, that'll be three dollars."

I handed over the money and asked: "Actually, can I have another one please?"

"No problem sir, that's another three dollars."

"Can I have one more?"

"Certainly sir, three more dollars please."

Smirking, I said: "I've just bought three watermelons for $9 but on your sign it says $10. Don't you realize how stupid you are?"

"That happens a lot," he chuckled, "until I point out that you just bought three watermelons instead of one."

In this chapter, I have elaborated on the most conventional pricing methods used by retail. That includes when and how to have a sale, how to discount, and how to increase prices.

Note: Retail pricing uses Manufacturer's Suggested Retail Price (MSRP). It is a much used tool in the auto market to show that the price is set by the big bad car companies and not the local car dealer.

1. The Most Effective Pricing Strategies

The different pricing strategies rated as most effective by the retailers in the Gartner study were discount, bundle, MSRP, odd pricing, price lining, and dynamic. For a full explanation of these see Chapter 9.

The survey found that a majority of respondents (51 percent) use software to manage product pricing; 39 percent of them use a stand-alone pricing application. Discount (advertising as below competition and bundle) were the most effective pricing strategies for the department, specialty, grocery, and e-commerce sectors, but advertised discounting took the lion's share of pricing strategy in every category.

Most interesting to us were the comments from the retailers on various strategies they use to increase sales and diminish inventory:

One retailer said his company used bundling, discount, price lining, and odd pricing for its online store. "We use different strategies because our customers are not just one solid segment of people in the market," he explained. Millennials, baby boomers, bargain hunters, and office managers are all groups targeted. "We use the different pricing strategies and then run them through a market analysis weekly," he said.

An example he gave: If the product is ink for a particular printer, the target market would consist of customers who purchased that printer in the past, which might include college students, accounting offices, or small businesses. Depending on which customers purchased the printer, different pricing strategies are used to attract them.

Bundling, he said, conveys a sense of value through the savings the customer receives on each item by buying in bulk. (For example, selling water bottles for $19.75 each, dropping the price to $18.76 per bottle when three or more are purchased.)

The retailer noted that while the discount strategy attracts aggressive bargain hunters to his business, it's not the most effective strategy on a per-customer basis, but it's still significant enough to his overall business to warrant its continued use.

The CEO and founder of a group of fashion retail stores said his stores use different pricing strategies to meet different goals. One such strategy, with the goal of selling more units, is incremental discounts that increase with the number of items purchased (e.g., getting 20 percent off the second item purchased and 30 percent off the third). The company also uses specific promotions to drive sales of items for which the store has large amounts in stock.

Because this retailer has high-end stores with name products, the concept of odd pricing, which implies bargain pricing, is not the perception he wants to create of his merchandise.

Everyday low prices, another common grocery price strategy used by stores such as Walmart and Target was included in the survey but is not among the strategies rated most effective by respondents because not everyone has the buying and pricing power of the giants.

A Canadian retailer reported that he uses Manufacturer's Suggested Retail Pricing (MSRP) in his online shop which sells vaporizers and related accessories. The MSRP, he said, allows him to maintain good relationships with manufacturers, but can be hard to maintain when the same products he sells show up at Amazon or eBay at lower prices. To avoid price wars, maintain good terms with manufacturers, and maintain its own margins, he developed a line of house brand accessories to pair with the core products sold at MSRP.

The bottom line is that when it comes to pricing technology, the most sophisticated, forward-looking global retail intelligence leaders offer Software as a Service (SaaS) based intelligence and analytics solutions that transform the way retailers price, select merchandise, and manage products in order to maximize sales and optimize margins.

2. Discounting and Sales

Discounting is a powerful tool to develop sales volumes. It is frequently misused and so I have included a section on how to have a successful sale.

Please don't have sales just because. Have a sale with an objective in mind: A measurable objective.

Never discount without purpose or else you are telling your customer that you are the low-cost provider and that bargain hunter is the type of customer you will attract. Can you offer savings greater than 15 percent? Any savings less than 10 percent will be ignored, unless you offer NO TAX sale days. No one likes to pay tax.

Are you having a sale to create a temporary surge in cash flow? Is it to purge some elderly inventory? Is it to attract a new demographic of customers?

Cinemas used to offer cheap nights on Tuesdays until Tuesdays became the biggest night of the week, cannibalizing more profitable sales during the balance of the week.

Other reasons for a sale may include a grand opening, to introduce new product, to create awareness during a slow period, or when going out of business.

3. Steps in Promotional Discount Pricing

Checklist 2 is a guide you can follow when running retail promotional discounts.

The idea is borrowed from John Winkler (*Pricing for Results*, Facts on File Publications, 1983) and is a light hearted look at applying the concepts of promotional discount pricing. It provides a guideline on spending, knitting together product lines, a surprise to keep everyone interested, and a rational order for a successful promotion.

Discounting is a strategy and to be successful, it must be carefully calibrated against measurable objectives. If you don't, then customers will wait for sale days and you won't get full prices. You may also develop a reputation as a low-cost provider and your margins will remain depressed.

4. Going from Analysis to Action: Implementing a Price Increase

Let us consider that you have done all the analytical work and found that your prices are low and are the cause of lost profitability. All avenues to reduce costs have been put under the microscope and explored and any improvements there will not lead to enough increase in profits.

What to do now? Obviously there is a call to action if all this high-level analytical work is not to be wasted. Do you then increase prices? What about the reaction of existing customers? What about your reputation in the industry? What about existing contract prices? Will your competition follow suit and raise prices or will they attack like a pack of ravenous wolves?

Checklist 2
Steps to Running Promotional Discount Pricing

Step 1: Decide your total advertising and promotion budget

- ☐ allocate dollars for basic expenses such as pamphlets and literature
- ☐ allocate dollars for theme advertising: all men's clothing for example, but not kids' shoes
- ☐ allocate dollars for promotional support to create awareness

Step 2: Divide the budget into sales cycles

- ☐ tie in with product support
- ☐ tie in advertising support
- ☐ tie in with sales aims

Step 3: In each period run 1 MAJOR promotion and 2 MINOR promotions. The minor programs are cheaper but keep creating awareness.

- ☐ discounts to new customers
- ☐ discounts to force existing volume
- ☐ payment, quantity, and standard discounts

Step 4: Negotiate in each period one big deal with one big customer

	Phase 1	Phase 2	Phase 3
Nuts	Heavy promotion	No promotion	Special price to trade only
Bolts	Competition to buyers	Free bolts as samples	No promotion
Screws	Discounts for display	Free screw with every washer	New product launch
Washers	No promotion	Combo-pack offer with screws	Buy 2 get 1 free

Most business owners would have nightmares about massive price hikes and the consequences of having existing customers leave them for the competition.

Justin Martin in "Raising prices, keeping customers" as published in the now defunct *Fortune Small Business* (September 13, 2007), tells a story of a businessman hesitant about raising prices. The company makes eight types of dry film lubricants and protective coatings. Clients included NASCAR drivers, professional drag racers, and monster-truckers, who use the products to keep their engines running smoothly. But the company, with prices fixed and costs climbing, was seeing the profit margin shrink at a rate of five percentage points a year. Finally after three years of price freezes, he was compelled to raise prices by 18 percent all at once.

Some customers left. But most stayed and there was an immediate boost on the bottom line and a jump in revenues from $2.6 million to just over $3 million.

The CEO later said he was surprised by how much leeway they had on what they charge.

So some customers will leave you. But it is not all bad. Consider the upside of increasing prices. Some customers will leave. They are the customers who are not loyal and buy only on price. It does not matter whether you are the only auto body shop in town that supplies a Ferrari as a loaner car; this type of customer does not care. So all the extra costs that you shoulder to offer a truly terrific service are a waste of money on that customer. Do you really need him? Is this a Mrs. Crabapple who drives up your costs?

Having concluded that the company's salvation lies only in increasing prices here are several implementation strategies in the next sections.

4.1 Increase prices

Jack up your prices. You could just be bloody-minded as David Jenkins of Kelowna explains. "I went through this years ago selling resin to the BC plywood industry. For years we had given them pricing based on raw material costs plus a small profit. Yes, it protected us from losing money but it in no way allowed us upward flexibility. It took a very hard stance on our part and a willingness to walk away from the business to get this changed."

4.2 Take time

Go slowly. A steady trickle of price increases is likely better received than a single torrent of increases. Increasing all your prices across the board by some massive number will probably work against your company. Better to have a series of small increases unevenly distributed across the spectrum of your products and services. A big increase will alert your competition and they could use it against you. A single big increase becomes the talk of the industry: "Did you hear that Anderson's just jacked up prices 45 percent yesterday?"

Let us consider this problem from the point of view of a distributor, a multifaceted service business, or a retail business. In these companies, the customers only really know the prices of ten items. Given sensitivity to a limited range of prices, there is scope with powerful enough software to sell belts or oil changes at different prices to different market segments. So the solution would be to listen to these customers and identify these ten items. With the right software you can begin the process of deconstructing your monolithic price list.

Warning: If your business is about to close its doors due to financial problems arising from low prices, you do not have the time to play games. Put the prices up today. The consequences of doing further testing and analyzing are that your business will fold. If you immediately implement a truly shocking price increase, some customers will leave, but the business may not fold today.

4.3 Say it's under review

A strategy of telling customers that prices are under review will be less shocking than a wholesale, unannounced, across-the-board increase. Customers will only care about or be sensitive to products and service increases that affect their business.

4.4 Unbundle

Can you unbundle your product or service?

If you have an item that normally sells for $45 as a kit, can you successfully take that kit apart and sell the components for higher prices and more profit overall? Could you, like a software vendor who offers full-service packages, offer to the price-sensitive customers a NO INCREASE package that strips away the services they do not use anyway but which add to your costs? (See Chapter 3 to review this.)

Similarly, can you bundle a single item or service with some add-on and charge more than the mere sum of its pieces? Your package would then change from a simple oil change to a 70-point check of the car's fluids and electrics. If you are a service company, offering a small upsell service can increase the dollar value of your overall product and decrease costs by reducing travel time. Or, if you are a bakery with an average $5 invoice per customer, adding a $2 package of cookies on each sale by positioning impulse cookies for sale by the cash register, lowers your cost per transaction and could be almost as effective as increasing prices.

Or consider this problem from the point of view of a company that does one thing or sells one product line, such as a car dealer. There are core prices — as advertised on TV! — leaving little wriggle room to simply hike up prices. So the change has to be in the add-on services or products that are a key part of the Unique Selling Proposition. If you are a plumber called out to a leaky faucet for example, the add-on would be an inspection of the overall under-sink plumbing and installing a replacement or new garburator. This does not necessarily raise prices but it does increase profit since the fixed costs of getting a person into the house are already paid leaving every extra profit dollar in your pocket.

4.5 Different pricing levels for different customers

Do you have to increase prices to all customers?

Consider that you have long time customers who buy 40 cases of your worm killer product each month and have done so, religiously, every year for a decade. Do your new customers who have been just now persuaded to use your worm killer, deserve the same level of pricing? Probably no, but how do you explain this to new customers? If they are willing to issue a purchase order committing to the purchase of 40 cases of worm killer product per month over the next ten years and pay on the 30th day, then perhaps they are deserving of the same pricing structure.

Years ago, I spoke with a fellow business analyst who explained that a company he had recently visited sold custom tanks each year to three customers. Two of the customers generated all the profit and the third customer — a huge multinational conglomerate — lost them all of the profit and more. The answer was obvious to me: They needed to stop selling to this huge customer or find a different pricing structure. But the client could not get past the thought of volunteering to let a third of his business go.

5. Price Lining

Price lining, also referred to as product line pricing, is a marketing process wherein products or services within a specific group are set at different price points. When the price is higher, the consumer perceives quality.

For example, a car may come in three different styles: a value model, a standard model, and a limited model. While each model has a different price point, the costlier model is seen as higher-end when compared to the base model, while both retain the same brand name.

Price lining offers consumers the flexibility of choice. Those seeking additional features or higher quality are willing to purchase the product at a higher price point, while budget-conscious shoppers or those that just want the basics may go for the lower-priced option. For a fuller explanation see Chapter 3 on Pricing for Startups.

6. Odd Pricing

Odd pricing is a psychological pricing method based on the belief that certain prices or price ranges are more appealing to buyers. This method involves setting a price in odd numbers (just under round even numbers) such as $49.95 instead of $50.00. Originally, this practice was meant to prevent pilfering of cash by forcing a cashier to open the cash register (charging $0.99 so the cashier would have to pay change to the customer) and thus register the transaction. Although not supported by any research findings, its proponents claim that the consumers see a $49.95 price as just above $40 and not as just below $50.

Worksheet 8 will help you as you plan a retail sale.

Worksheet 8
Retail: ~~How~~ to ~~Have~~ a Sale

This is a guide you can follow when running retail promotional discounts.

Caution: Never have a sale without an objective in mind. Are you having a sale to introduce a new product? Are you having a sale to reduce surplus or old inventory? Are you having a sale to attract new customers? Are you having a sale to remind people you are still in the marketplace?

What is the purpose of your sale and how are you going to measure its success?

What is your total advertising and promotion budget?

How much will you spend on basic expenses such as pamphlets, banners, social media?

What portion of your allocation will be spent on theme advertising: all men's clothing for example, but not kids' shoes.

What portion of your advertising dollars will be spent to create awareness? Radio? TV? Newspapers? Online?

In each period run 1 MAJOR promotion and 2 MINOR promotions. The minor programs are cheaper but keep creating awareness. These could be:

- discounts to new customers
- discounts to force existing volume
- payment terms, quantity, and standard discounts

Worksheet 8 — Continued

Major promotion: product or service

Minor promotion 1:

Minor promotion 2:

EXAMPLE:

This table shows a three-part promotional cycle combining opportunity and timing to buy.

	Phase 1	Phase 2	Phase 3
Nuts	Heavy promotion to the general public	No promotion	Special price to trade only
Bolts	Prize to heavy industrial buyers	Free bolts as samples	No promotion
Screws	Discounts for buying a counter display	Free screw with every washer	New product launch
Washers	No promotion	Combo pack offer with screws	Buy 2 get 1 free

Chapter 11
Pricing Conclusions and Steps to Profit

This chapter is a commandment to you as a business owner. Do something about your pricing; do anything. Remember that even a dead fish can float downstream.

I have tried my very best to list the following sections in the order of steps which will benefit a businessperson in the most logical and least time consuming way. Following these steps can help make your company into a profit leader.

1. Sell Your Price and Reap the Benefits

By far the most constructive use of your time will be to train yourself and your sales staff to sell your price. In Chapter 2 on selling your dream price, I lay out a large number of ways to help you to get your price and not have to discount. Every dollar discounted comes off your bottom line, so not offering discounts will immediately — on your first sale — improve your profits.

2. Stop Discounting: It Kills Profits

Price in three packages: DREAM, VALUE FOR MONEY, and SAVE THE SALE pricing. Every time you are compelled to drop the price, you should remove something of value to the customer and thereby maintain your margins while saving the sale.

3. Cut Your Price Waterfall Costs

Take a harsh look at what you give away for free. What is free now could be a revenue stream that will improve your profits. See my reference to LinkedIn in section 9. in Chapter 9, and use Worksheet 9.

4. Spend Time Developing Your USP and Branding

Your competition can learn to sell their prices as well and will follow you. The value of a UNIQUE Selling Proposition (USP) — in the true meaning of unique as being the one and only — is that it becomes sustainable. This is your *Star Trek* moment to chart a path for your business where no one will dare to follow.

5. Pay Obsessive Attention to Customer Service and Quality

In *The Loyalty Connection* (magellan-solutions.com/wp-content/uploads/2014/09/SecretstoCustomerRetentionandIncreasedProfits.pdf, accessed March, 2019) we saw that customers will leave because of poor customer service and poor quality work in priority over pricing problems. So, if clients want great quality and unsurpassed customer service, why not work hard to develop that and stand out in the crowd as the company that makes customers happy? Be the go-to provider!

6. Develop a System to Review Your Prices and Apply Frequently

A great pricing strategy can work for years but it is not static. In this book I outlined more than one strategy and you may have to deploy all of them over time, some of them all at once. Like any good business person, monitor, tweak, and monitor again, in a cycle.

7. Build, Track, and Analyze Your Data

Walmart collects masses of data, why not you? This is a data world and having reliable data can help you make the right decisions. What data should you collect?

You already know everything about the costs of your product or service but realistically you know nothing about the demand for the product.

Worksheet 9
The Price Waterfall (or How Profits Drain Away)

Do you have off-invoice costs that cripple your profitability? Below is a list of costs; far from comprehensive but perhaps it will help you to consider costs carefully.

Do you offer free delivery?

Deduct that number from your profits	$ _____
Deduct free installation	$ _____
Deduct free consultation	$ _____
Deduct free support after the purchase	$ _____
Deduct dealer discounts	$ _____
Deduct volume discounts	$ _____
Deduct salesperson discounts to get the deal	$ _____
Deduct 1.2% for early payment	$ _____
Deduct money cost of 60–90 day terms	$ _____
Deduct co-op advertising	$ _____
Deduct merchandising program	$ _____
Deduct annual volume rebates	$ _____
Deduct all from invoice price to see what your profits really are	$ _____

Are the discounts applied on the basis of some data or just gut feel?

☐ Yes   ☐ No

How many of these costs can be eliminated or charged to the customer?   _____

Every promotion and sales pitch should be measured to establish customer response to the product and to the price.

More data = better decisions.

8. Keep Going

Pricing is part of marketing and not a part of accounting. Successful companies find the market first and then the product or service after.

The pricing methods in common use and which you may have used for years lead to mediocrity at best. Certainly, these methods leave money on the table. Big companies have for years improved profits by seeing and developing pricing as a strategy for profit engineering and not just to improve sales. They price for profit, not sales.

When a consumer is presented with an opportunity to open his or her wallet, and there has been no clear exposition of what the value is to be exchanged for dollars, then the only way to measure value is dollars per hour or dollars per unit. Weak salespeople and weak companies default to this way of doing business and wonder why their margins are so low and they struggle to make a profit.

If value is presented clearly and vibrantly, through the Unique Selling Proposition, and before the price is mentioned, then the decision is NOT dollars per unit or per hour but rather on the value to the customer. This is the way to get your price and improve profits.

The other piece of the jigsaw puzzle is choice. In this book I have tried to show the value of choice in helping a consumer to make a decision. In this world we are pushed daily to buy something and our range of free will is narrowing. Being offered only one price is a take it or leave it proposition. Two prices is better but is still a bit of a straitjacket. Three choices is the maximum number I recommend, because beyond this lies decision paralysis and no sale will come of that.

If we present value well and then offer choices to fit the three possible budgets of a potential client, we have made the decision to buy simpler.

Finally, you should remember to sell for profit, not revenues or a mere sales increase. You can't eat sales but you can eat profits.

Chapter 12

How to Price: A Workbook Approach

The question most asked of me when I give speeches on pricing is how to price a particular product or service. Clearly this is beyond the scope of a ten-minute review, or even after having seen a quick demonstration of eight different methods in use today. While there is no definite answer to identify that your product must be sold for $41.95 for example, you can find a best approximation by using a process approach.

The purpose of this chapter is to show eight steps to finding your price. This process is not a silver bullet any more than creating a great sales program is a silver bullet. It takes time and effort and needs frequent testing to keep it effective.

The steps in this workbook approach are: position your company, pick a niche market, put value first, frame your price, create your DREAM price, collect customer data, understand your marketing environment, and be brave.

1. Step 1: Make a Decision to Position Your Company

Are you intentionally a low-cost provider competing in the middle of the road with people all screaming that they have the lowest prices?

Then, pay attention to the price waterfall and pocket price banding (for a simple example, look at the Castle Battery case study in Chapter 13) that can open profit doors for you.

Are you the go-to company with high prices and great service? In this instance, pay attention to the two things that matter to customers more than prices: great customer service and great quality. These will drive up your costs. Remember to put value on the table before prices are introduced and work hard to keep good customers.

2. Step 2: Pick a Niche Market

Don't plan to compete in the middle of the market where the big companies play. Playing in the middle of the road will only get you run over. See Chapter 3 on pricing for start-ups. Profit can be made in the niche markets, the sides of the market ignored by the companies trying to build market share.

3. Step 3: Put Value First and State It

Your Unique Selling Proposition is a sentence or phrase that explains what makes you special. It gives your prospective customers a reason to do business with you rather than your competitors.

When developing your USP, it is important that you put yourself in your prospects' position. Look at your product or service from the point of view of someone thinking about buying it. What is important to your potential customer?

Most companies have a rotten USP: "We have great service and our customers love us," tells you nothing and at heart, this company competes on price.

However, "Six days a week we install the most reliable hot water tanks on the south side" at least paints a picture that a potential customer can grasp in a few seconds. Tell your customers your USP: on the phone, your invoices, your websites, letterhead, on quotes, everywhere.

4. Step 4: Frame Your Price around Your Competitors' Prices

What do your competitors charge for the identical or near-identical product or service? You need to know this because your industry is always in the grip of its most unintelligent competitor. If competitors are driving down prices, customers will make unfortunate comparisons until you tell them otherwise.

Knowing all of your competitors is key and the effort to make a comparison will make you more aware of where you fit in the pecking order. Are you in the middle, top, or bottom band in the pricing marketplace? Are your products and service easily comparable? Is it easy for customers to compare what you and your competitors offer, or is the picture so muddy that they default to looking at dollars per unit? Knowing this helps you frame your price. See Chapter 7 on customer perceptions and behavior.

5. Step 5: Create Your Dream Price

If you have read references in this book to the role of choice, you know already that you need three prices. You need a dream price: This is the price you would love to get and may in the right circumstances get. It has dozens of features that convey real benefits to the buyer when purchased and will give the buyer some bragging rights.

Let's recap: The value for money (standard) price is where you will likely make the most sales, where the margins are good and make your accountant happy. This price level has the same features and benefits as the dream price but with some key, cost-reducing features removed.

The last price is the save the sale price designed to suit those clients with thin wallets. This level has fewer features and benefits than the value for money price and much fewer than the DREAM price. Your margins are good but the job size or invoice size is smaller. You cannot survive on a steady diet of save the sale jobs.

Don't discount without removing features: The value for money price is lower because the product or service has fewer benefits than the dream price. The save the sale price is lower than either because it has the fewest benefits.

6. Step 6: Collect Data

This is a data-driven world and too many small businesses do not collect information on their existing or potential customers.

In "Command Manufactures Success through Communication," *Business Examiner* (July, 2015), the owners of Command Industries admit their shock after quizzing their customers. A mentor had suggested that they speak directly with their top customers and ask them, why do you buy from Command? "I was sure the answers were going to be pricing-related and focused on comparing costs with our competitors." said Rob Woudwijk. "But the results of those conversations shocked me. It was never about the money. Instead they talked about the way we communicated with them, the level of transparency and honesty we have as a company and our problem solving mentality."

Successful businesses know with exactness the wants, wishes, and buying behaviors of specific customers. They have analyzed the size of the market or the number of potential customers that fit the target profile. Further still, they know their customers' names, ages, genders, incomes, home and Internet addresses, professions, education, associations, and marital status, number of children, hobbies, their tastes and interests. They grasp what their customers watch, read, and hear. They understand their likes and dislikes. They understand the buying cycle and the market fluctuations. Knowing a customer to this depth is one of the key characteristics of highly successful business leaders.

For most business owners, their target market is as faceless as a telephone book and their marketing efforts as effective as snail mailing everyone under the letter P.

Even knowing what your customer is going to do with your product or service can point you to higher profits. As a wily business owner, you must know what benefit your customer is trying to solve by buying your product or service.

If the product is a chop saw and the weekend warrior is in your store, the salesperson's first question has to be, "What project are you planning?" If the project is a small cabinet, the cheapest machine will be satisfactory. If the customer is making his living with the chop saw, a durable, reliable machine is the ticket.

If your market is upwardly mobile, there might be an element of keeping up with the Joneses or one-upmanship in the market. More highly priced products carry a cachet of being more successful – if you position yourself by your marketing and branding. When Tynan water got its signature blue glass bottles on a Bond film, sales rocketed in a category crowded with high-priced water.

So, create a table of what you and your sales staff think is the customer profile using the points above. List all characteristics and then start ranking them in importance. To fine tune this process, collect information on your customers. See Worksheet 10.

I am still astonished how few businesses collect even elementary data such as phone numbers and email addresses. With social media

Worksheet 10
Strategic Considerations

Part 1: Your Customers

If you already have customers, be brave and ask them why they buy from you.

You could ask questions such as:

a.) How important is quality to you? What experiences have you had in the past with other suppliers?

b.) How important is timeliness to you? What experiences have you had in the past with other suppliers?

c.) What customer service aspects are important to you?

d.) What happened to your last supplier?

Part 2: Your Competitors

What do your competitors charge, and for what? This is a competitive analysis and can reflect everything from opening hours to the age of their vehicles, years in business, to number of complaints on Google.

Competitor	Strengths	Weaknesses	Price

you can keep your company in front of customers and potential customers, constantly testing the waters with product offerings and sales.

When you have finished, test, test, test, and then start again. This is work, but is directly related to sales and sales growth. As above, this is a habit of a successful businessperson.

7. Step 7: Be Aware of Your Marketing Environment

You may have heard of the French Paradox. In 1991, researchers tried to explain the low incidence of heart disease in France, where everyone ate lots of fatty foods (e.g., butter, cream, cheese). The solution to this conundrum, the investigators claimed, was that the French drank red wine and this was put forth as a scientific sounding explanation.

The French wine exporters pounced on this and ran full page ads in US newspapers crowing about the positive health impact of a glass of red a day. Sales soared. Prices rose. A similar pattern emerged each time when oat bran, yogurt, alkaline water, and echinacea were highlighted as health givers.

In February of 2015, Terry Reilly, of the CBC radio show *Under the Influence* aired a tremendously insightful examination of the impact of weather on sales (www.cbc.ca/radio/undertheinfluence/how-weather-affects-marketing-1.2801774, accessed May, 2019). In this episode, O'Reilly describes how the people behind The Weather Network convinced Campbell's Soup to exploit a small bump in chicken noodle soup sales when the weather turned rotten. Instead of just letting it happen, the weather network fed information to Campbell's to enable them to advertise chicken noodle soup heavily three days before bad weather hit and made people miserable. The result? A tremendous bump in sales.

Consider the price of champagne. Champagne is fizzy white wine, when all is said and done. It costs marginally more to make but sells for a significantly higher price. Why? Because the manufacturers have convinced us all that a meaningful celebration of life, success, marriage, sometimes divorce, graduation, birth, and any Hallmark holiday can only be celebrated properly with a bottle of bubbly. The producers have "welded" champagne to the celebration buying environment.

These are three instances of a marketing environment affecting price. In the first, an accidental but favorable review was pounced upon to drive sales and prices. In the second instance, data mining was used to exploit a changing mood and bump sales, although not in this instance, price. In the third instance, the manufacturers set out from the beginning to convince us to pay more for their market segmented, highly differentiated, USP-driven product.

So the final part of your work must be to include these marketing environments that influence your pricing. What do you control? What can you influence? What factors put you in the driver's seat? Even the tiniest thing can make you master of your universe and the price driver in your marketplace.

8. Step 8: Don't Be Afraid to Experiment

There are just too many stories of products that did not sell UNTIL the price was seriously cranked up. Price is often an indicator of quality and value in customers' minds.

Researchers at the university in Wisconsin concluded that the problem with the local wine industry was that the producers were afraid to charge for the value of the wine offered.

Chapter 13
True-Life Business Scenarios

This chapter will discuss some case studies.

In the first case study, taken from the Harvard Business Review, the company has a classic case of profits bleeding away due to off-invoice costs that are not recovered. Attention to these seemingly minor matters yielded a massive increase in profitability.

In the second case study, taken from the author's own consulting experience, the company was cash short because it had failed to use its systems to keep a firm hand on a growing mountain of unusable repair parts.

1. Pocket Price Banding: Castle Battery Company Case

The following, somewhat disguised, case shows how one company used the pocket price waterfall and band to identify profit leaks and regain control of its pricing system. It illustrates one way in which the waterfall and band concepts can be applied, and shows how, if a company doesn't manage its pricing policies on all levels, experienced customers may be working those policies to their own advantage.

The Castle Battery Company is a manufacturer of replacement lead-acid batteries for automobiles. Castle's direct customers are auto parts distributors, auto parts retailers, and some general mass merchandisers. With return on sales averaging in the 7% range, Castle's profitability is very sensitive to even small improvements in price: A 1% increase in price with no volume loss, for instance, would increase operating profit dollars by 14%.

Extreme overcapacity in the battery industry and gradual commoditization made it increasingly difficult for Castle to distinguish its products from competitors. So Castle senior management was skeptical that there was much, if any, potential for price improvement. However, Castle managers had entirely overlooked lucrative pricing opportunities at the transaction level.

Figure 14 shows the typical pocket price waterfall for one of Castle's common battery models, the Power-Lite, sold to an auto parts retailer. From a base price of $28.40, Castle deducted standard dealer/distributor and order-size discounts. The company also subtracted an on-invoice exception discount, negotiated on a customer-by-customer basis to "meet competition." With these discounts, the invoice price to the retailer totaled $21.16. What little transaction price monitoring that Castle did focused exclusively on invoice.

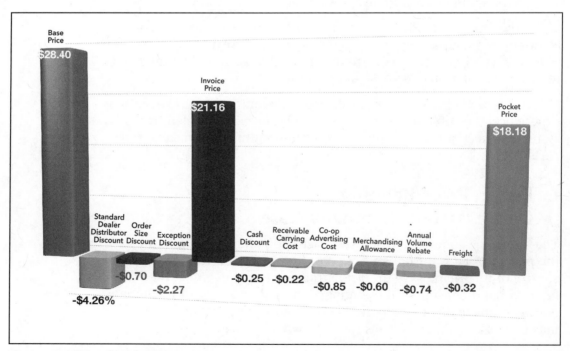

Figure 14: Off-invoice Discounts

That focus ignored a big part of the pricing picture: off-invoice discounting. Castle allowed cash discounts of 1.2% for timely payments by accounts. Additionally, the company granted extended terms (payment not required until 60 or 90 days after receipt of a shipment) as part of promotional programs or on an exception basis. For this transaction, the extra cost of carrying these extended receivables totaled 22 cents. Cooperative advertising, where Castle contributed to its accounts' local advertising of Castle products, cost 85 cents. A special merchandising program in effect at the time of this transaction discounted another 60 cents. An annual volume rebate, based on total volume and paid at year end, decreased revenues by yet another 74 cents; and freight paid by Castle for shipping the battery to the retailer cost 32 cents.

The invoice price minus this long list of off-invoice items resulted in a pocket price of only $18.18, a full 14% less than invoice. The total revenue drop from base price down to pocket price is the "pocket discount" — in this case, $10.22, of which $2.98 was off-invoice.

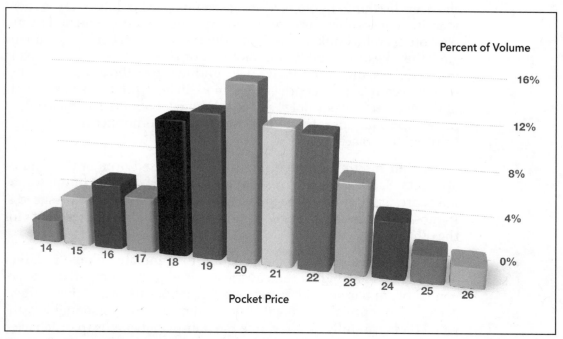

Figure 15: A Single Product Can Have a Wide Product Price Band

Castle managers, perplexed by the scatter of pocket prices by account size, launched an immediate investigation. In most cases, they found no legitimate reason why certain low-volume accounts were paying such discounted prices. Often, they discovered that these accounts were unusually experienced and clever accounts — customers who had been dealing with Castle for 20 years or more and who knew just whom to call at Castle headquarters to get that extra exception discount, that percentage point of additional co-op advertising, that extra 30 or 60 days to pay. These favorite old accounts were granted extra discounts based on familiarity and relationships rather than on economic justification. These experienced clients understood Castle's pocket price waterfall and were working it against the company.

Castle senior management realized that its transaction pricing process was out of control, that decision making up and down the waterfall lacked discipline, and that no one was focusing on the comprehensive total of those decisions. The end result was a pricing reality that didn't square with Castle's strategy of rewarding account size with lower prices, and that was costing Castle millions.

To correct its transaction pricing situation, Castle mounted a three-part program. First, it took very aggressive corrective actions to bring the over discounted, "old favorite" accounts back in line. Management identified the problem accounts and explained the situation and its impact on overall company profits to the sales force. Then the company gave the sales force nine months to fix or drop those outliers. Fixing meant decreasing the excessive discounting across the waterfall so that outlier accounts' pocket prices were more in line with those of accounts of similar size. Salespeople who couldn't negotiate their outlier pocket prices up to an appropriate level were to find other accounts in their territory to replace them.

Within the time allotted, the sales force fixed 90% of the trouble accounts. Sales' newfound realization that every element of the waterfall represented a viable negotiating lever contributed to this success. In most cases, the salespeople easily found profitable replacements for the other 10%.

Second, Castle launched a program to stimulate volume in larger accounts that had higher than average pocket prices compared with accounts of similar size. Management singled out the attractive "target" accounts for special treatment. Sales and marketing personnel investigated them carefully to determine the non-price benefits to which each was most sensitive. The company increased volume in these accounts not by lowering price but by delivering the specific benefits that were most important to each: higher service levels for some, shortened order lead times for others, more frequent sales calls for still others.

Finally, Castle embarked on a crash program to get the transaction pricing process back under control. This program included, among other components, setting clear decision rules for each discretionary item in the waterfall. For example, the company capped exception discounts at 5% and granted them only after a specific volume and margin impact evaluation. Management also set up new information systems to guide and monitor transaction pricing decisions. And Castle established pocket price as the universal measure of price performance in all of these systems. It began to track and assign, transaction-by-transaction, all of the significant off-invoice waterfall elements that were previously collected and reported only on a company-wide basis. Further, pocket price realization became a major component of the incentive, compensation of salespeople, sales managers, and product managers.

Castle reaped rich and sustained rewards from these three transaction pricing initiatives. In the first year, average pocket price levels increased 3% and, even though volume remained flat, operating profits swelled 4%. The company realized additional pocket price gains in each of the two subsequent years.

Castle also received some unexpected strategic benefits from its newfound transaction pricing capability. Account-specific pocket price reporting revealed a small but growing distribution channel where Castle pocket prices were consistently higher than average. Increasing volume and penetration in this emerging channel became one of Castle's key strategic initiatives this past year. The fresh and more detailed business perspective that Castle senior managers gained from their transaction pricing involvement became the catalyst for an ongoing stream of similar strategic insights.

— *HARVARD BUSINESS REVIEW* September – October 1992

2. GENERIC Truck and Diesel Ltd.
"Re-setting the Clock"

March 11, 2005, Overview

In essence, GENERIC Truck and Diesel is a business worth salvaging for its ability to generate a retirement nest egg for the owners. Its past ten years of poor financial performance can easily be turned around and it can again be made into a profitable business, even in the current economic climate. If the economy revives in the Main City to Smallville corridor, local companies overall will be busy again.

I have not answered anywhere in this report why the company got into trouble. That is not important. The company's history shows us what not to repeat. Nevertheless, the staff are certain whom to blame and the loss of trust in the current management and ownership is serious. To remedy that, some of my recommendations are personnel based. In brief, this company can no longer be a family concern in order to operate and be sold profitably. The company needs to embrace the best methods employed by modern companies to cut out the non-performing bits and forge ahead armed with a plan.

This plan falls into two parts:

1. Bandages: What needs to be done immediately with regards to reforming the parts department, the service department, personnel, and getting basic business information in front of the owner.

2. Treatment: The longer term business systems projects that enhance profits and codify procedures and methods. Codifying means that any outsider can buy and run the business with minimum training, thereby enhancing the business selling price.

Parts Department, Analysis

1. The parts department is untidy and dirty enough to make it a difficult place to work and truly discouraging for the staff. I had expected, with the low volumes that the shelves would be organized and tidy.

2. There is $45,000 worth of dead stock from Supplier Z alone. The dead stock is the result of inattention by the parts department and means that $45,000 of cash was taken from GENERIC Truck's bottom line with no return on that investment. With 40% margins before the parts labor is added, the dead stock value translates into countless lost dollars in over-the-counter sales and repair jobs. This amount of dead stock has grown to this level from zero after the building burned.

3. Although the parts manager was diligent on the single purchase order I saw completed, the other staff and Miss A. have informed that this is not usually the case. While the current COD basis for buying parts is in place, poor paperwork procedures have no impact other than creating unnecessary confusion in the parts department (no names and prices). Soon this paperwork will be needed for cash-flow projections.

4. The backorder system in Rinax is not used leading to confusion over what is ordered for whom, when it will be in, and creating a dependence on someone's memory.

5. Parts leave the building without being charged. Given the dire financial straits in which the company finds itself, this is outrageous and totally unnecessary.

6. Anecdotally, I was told that customers occasionally leave the building with parts charged on their accounts when they should have been paying cash. Rinax must be able to link together the accounts receivable and invoicing systems to stop this happening.

7. There was a $20,000 variance in the inventory at last count. This information came from the parts manager and I did not verify this. This number is too high and is a further indicator of sloppy controls. A variance of 1 to 5 % is appropriate in a parts department.

8. The parts department does not up-sell to customers. It has no notion of its breakeven sales volume, so it operates in a vacuum. The breakeven according to the October 31 figures is $19,567 per week including sales to the service department.

9. The conflicts that exist between the parts department and the service department are destructive if understandable in the company's current situation. Service blames the parts for poor performance and has only a dim understanding of the cash constraints. Most importantly the service department believes the parts staff think of them as an annoyance as opposed to a partner in the business.

10. The staff complain that the parts manager is absent when needed, indeed absent too much.

Solutions

1. Clean up the parts shelves.

2. Tighter inventory controls. Items that will become dead stock will always be purchased. That is part of being in the parts business. However, Supplier Z and other vendors will take back inventory under certain terms and conditions and time frames. The parts department needs to be vigilant about this number — the dollar value of inventory over 270 days — and present this figure to the owner monthly on his wall whiteboard. Together with the number of days old that the inventory is, and the dollar value of cores and warranty parts not yet returned, this will give the owner all the information he needs to see that the parts department is controlling the cash outlay.

3. When the purchasing elbow room is created to buy parts inventory again, only the fastest moving "A" parts should be purchased for the first six months. This will guarantee that the room created by the returns and new financial picture are maximized. Purchases of items NOT on the "A" list should be treated as special

order and a 70% deposit collected to cover the cost of the parts (60% of the sale value) and freight. Moreover, when the part arrives, it should be immediately invoiced to the customer and the bill sent out. This will improve cash flow.

4. In the longer term, the parts department needs to use the Rinax backorder system to control parts ordered for customers. The backorder system is needed to create credibility with customers and its immediate activation will be simpler now than when the department gets really busy again. When the system is underway, the backorder report needs to be printed weekly and reviewed by the owner and the parts manager. The total length of the report is the first indicator to the owner about whether the parts department is doing its job. The second indicator is the age of the backorders.

5. Purchase orders filled out completely need to go to accounting as input into the cash-flow figures. Purchases of $20,000 this week on purchase orders means that in some 30 days the company must be able to write a check for $20,000 and the finance department needs to know this in advance.

6. When the purchase orders start becoming useful input to the cash-flow figures, the finance department's weekly cash-flow meetings can produce a weekly budget figure for the parts department. Armed with a budget, the parts manager can afford to buy nonessentials for the add-on sales.

7. Uncharged parts. The service and parts department can work together better to control parts leaving the building. Currently the service manager chases down what he hopes was used on the work orders because nothing is written down on the work order. I suggest strongly that the mechanic take the work order from the gray table to the parts counter so that the parts man can write the part on the work order while it is fresh in his mind. No work order, no parts.

8. A paperwork flow chart will unearth the areas where the systems have holes, where unnecessary steps are taken, and where unnecessary paper is kept.

9. Variance in inventory can be brought under control by counting the inventory more often, I suggest that the entire inventory be verified as soon as is possible and that, biweekly, some part of the inventory is counted to verify the numbers. The dollar value is important but more importantly, and peculiar to parts businesses, having nine pieces of ten cent c clips on the shelf instead of the ten your mechanic or customer needs to finish a job is

critical. Counting some portion of the inventory at regular intervals becomes habit forming after awhile, fills the slow periods, increases confidence in the validity of the numbers you see on screen, and makes all stock taking easier. The owner needs to see that all the divisions of the inventory are counted regularly by a report from the parts manager showing the variance and what date each section was counted.

10. Pricing issues. If the service department charges parts at a 15% premium on average, this will add $102,198 dollars to the bottom line generating a profit of 5%. The owner needs to keep this number in front of the service manager's face at all items to make certain that it happens.

11. Walmart pricing, otherwise known as ROI pricing, is a tactic to create extra profits and margins while also creating the impression of being the cheapest source in town. The same tactics can be used to help the owner or the forthcoming salesperson to buy back old customers and up sell. The tactic should, for the moment, be used only on consumable items where the owner can say to the customer, buy 10 cases and get one free without impact on the margins.

12. The owner can help the parts department focus on its job by posting the breakeven dollar volume for the department to see and referring to it often. This figure needs to be reviewed to keep it true and accurate. This focus will also help morale in the service department because the parts department will start seeing the service department as customers and contributors to its weekly targets instead of an annoyance.

13. The company needs a sales[person] other than the owner. The owner's skills and presence is needed in the company with attention first to the parts department and then the service department. As parts become available again, the owner can train a salesperson to make the rounds.

In this example, a parts and service company found itself in trouble and, like many companies, let its controls and metrics lapse. My 3-day review of the situation, partly reproduced here, focuses on rebuilding those controls and finding areas — some small — where money was to be found. Pricing and adding value play a large part of this study.

Best of all, was finding that the parts department was in total disarray and was sitting atop $30,000 worth of items that could be exchanged for a substantial credit with its major supplier, thereby creating operating capital.

Download Kit

Please enter the URL you see in the box below into your computer web browser to access and download the kit.

www.self-counsel.com/updates/dapricing/19kit.htm

The download kit includes:

- Worksheets from the book
- Checklists for you to follow as you price your products or services
- — And more!